POSTER COLLECTION
TYPO CHINA

13

AF723930

Mit einem Essay von/Essay by Eva Lüdi Kong

MUSEUM FÜR GESTALTUNG ZÜRICH
PLAKATSAMMLUNG/POSTER COLLECTION

LARS MÜLLER PUBLISHERS

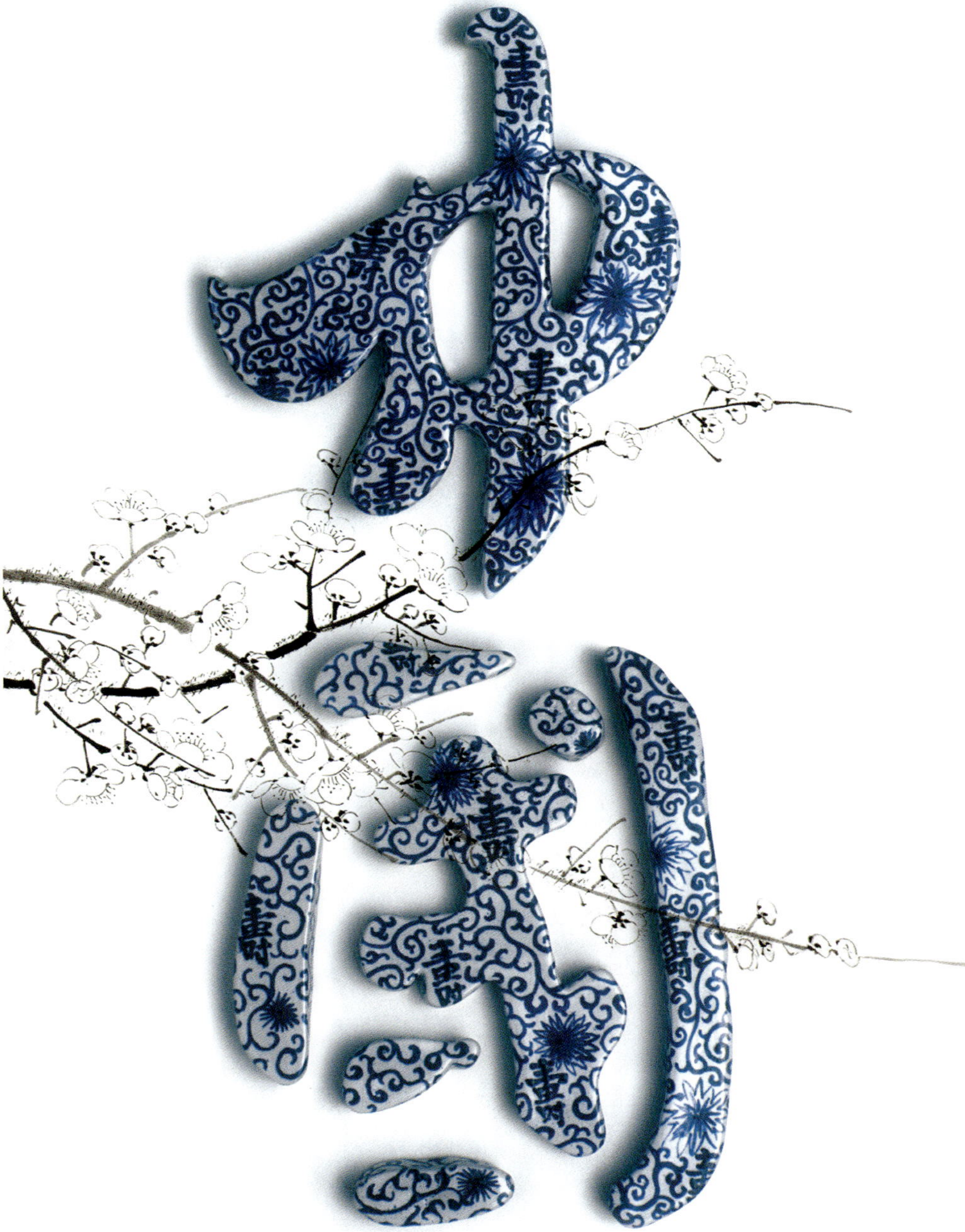

1 **He Jianping**
China
中國
2005

VORWORT

Die Anregung des Gestalters He Jianping zu dieser Publikation liess uns nicht lange zögern, denn schon seit längerem hatten chinesische Plakate unsere Aufmerksamkeit geweckt, die der ideologisch bedingten Erstarrung auf wohltuende Art widersprachen. Wenn die Entwicklung des Plakats in Hongkong und Taiwan gegenüber der Volksrepublik einen Vorsprung hat, so ist es aufs Ganze gesehen doch eine sehr junge Erscheinung, die ohne die Umwälzungen der letzten Jahre nicht denkbar wäre. Seit dem Ende der 1990er Jahre sind in China verschiedene internationale Plakatwettbewerbe entstanden, an denen sich die Gestalter auch dem westlichen Urteil aussetzen wollen. Wie auffallend häufig sie in ihren Plakaten die Schrift zur Hauptsache machen, lässt den Wunsch erkennen, mit dem einzigartigen Reichtum der eigenen Schriftkultur am Puls der Zeit zu sein. Nicht nur darum schien es uns gerechtfertigt, die Auswahl auf typografische Plakate zu konzentrieren. Die chinesische Schrift verfügt über eine Visualität und eine semantische Vielschichtigkeit, die die Möglichkeiten unseres Alphabets weit überbieten.

Die Begeisterung, mit der unserem Aufruf gefolgt wurde, neue Arbeiten einzusenden, lässt die Vitalität einer noch kleinen Gruppe von jungen Gestaltern erahnen, die die Mechanismen des internationalen Wettbewerbs entdecken. Es ist bezeichnend, dass viele der gezeigten Plakate im Eigenauftrag entstanden sind, weil es in China noch an Auftraggebern und somit an einer realen Plakatkultur fehlt. Diese Auswahl ist darum ebenso willkommen wie vorläufig und entspricht unserem Blick auf das «booming China», der aufmerksam skeptisch und hoffnungsvoll ist.

Dass wir angesichts chinesischer Typografie einer Faszination erliegen, die sich auch durch Unkenntnis nährt, braucht nicht betont zu werden. Chinesischer Text vermittelt sich uns oft nur als Textur, weil es an anspruchsvoller Übersetzungsarbeit fehlt, die notwendig wäre, um die Plakate in ihrer Aussagekraft zu würdigen.

Können wir diesen Arbeiten also überhaupt gerecht werden, wenn wir sie auf die gewohnte Augenhöhe unserer Selektion heben? Ja, wenn wir dazu die Spielregeln eines Plakatwettbewerbs annehmen wollen. Denn auch dort machen wir aus dem, was wir sehen *sollen*, das, was wir sehen *wollen*. Und jedes Plakat operiert auch dort mit dem Kalkül wechselseitiger Klischees und Erwartungen. Was zum Wesen eines Plakats gehört, kommt den positiven Missverständnissen ideal entgegen: Ein Plakat will zunächst und vor allem *gesehen* werden, nicht gelesen.

Felix Studinka

FOREWORD

We did not hesitate for long when the designer He Jianping suggested this publication: Chinese posters had caught our attention some time before, as a satisfying contradiction of ideologically driven rigidity. The development of the poster in Hongkong and Taiwan may be ahead of the People's Republic, but seen overall this is a very recent phenomenon, unthinkable without the upheavals of recent years. Various international poster competitions have been instituted in China since the late 1990s, and here the designers want to lay themselves open to Western judgement as well. It is striking how frequently their posters focus on the characters, showing their desire to keep up with the times in terms of the unique richness of their own typographical culture. This was not the only reason why it seemed right to us to concentrate on choosing typographical posters. Chinese characters have a visual quality and a semantic complexity that go far beyond the possibilities our alphabet affords.

Our appeal to submit new works met with considerable enthusiasm. This gives a sense of the vitality of a group, small as yet, of young designers who are discovering international competition mechanisms. It is typical that many of the posters shown were produced on the designers' own initiative, because China still lacks clients who are prepared to commission posters, and thus has no real poster culture. So this selection is as welcome as it is provisional, and fits in with our attentively sceptical yet hopeful view of "booming China".

It goes without saying that the fascination with Chinese typography we have succumbed to is fed on ignorance. Chinese text often affects us simply as a texture, because we do not have the necessary translations skills to be aware of the posters' expressive quality.

So can we do justice to these posters at all if we submit them to our usual selective scrutiny? Yes, if we are prepared to play by poster competition rules. For there too we make what we *should* see into what we *want* to see. And there too every poster operates by taking mutual clichés and expectations into account. Something that is part of the essence of a poster is always the perfect concession to positive misunderstandings: a poster is intended first and foremost to be *seen*, not read.

Felix Studinka

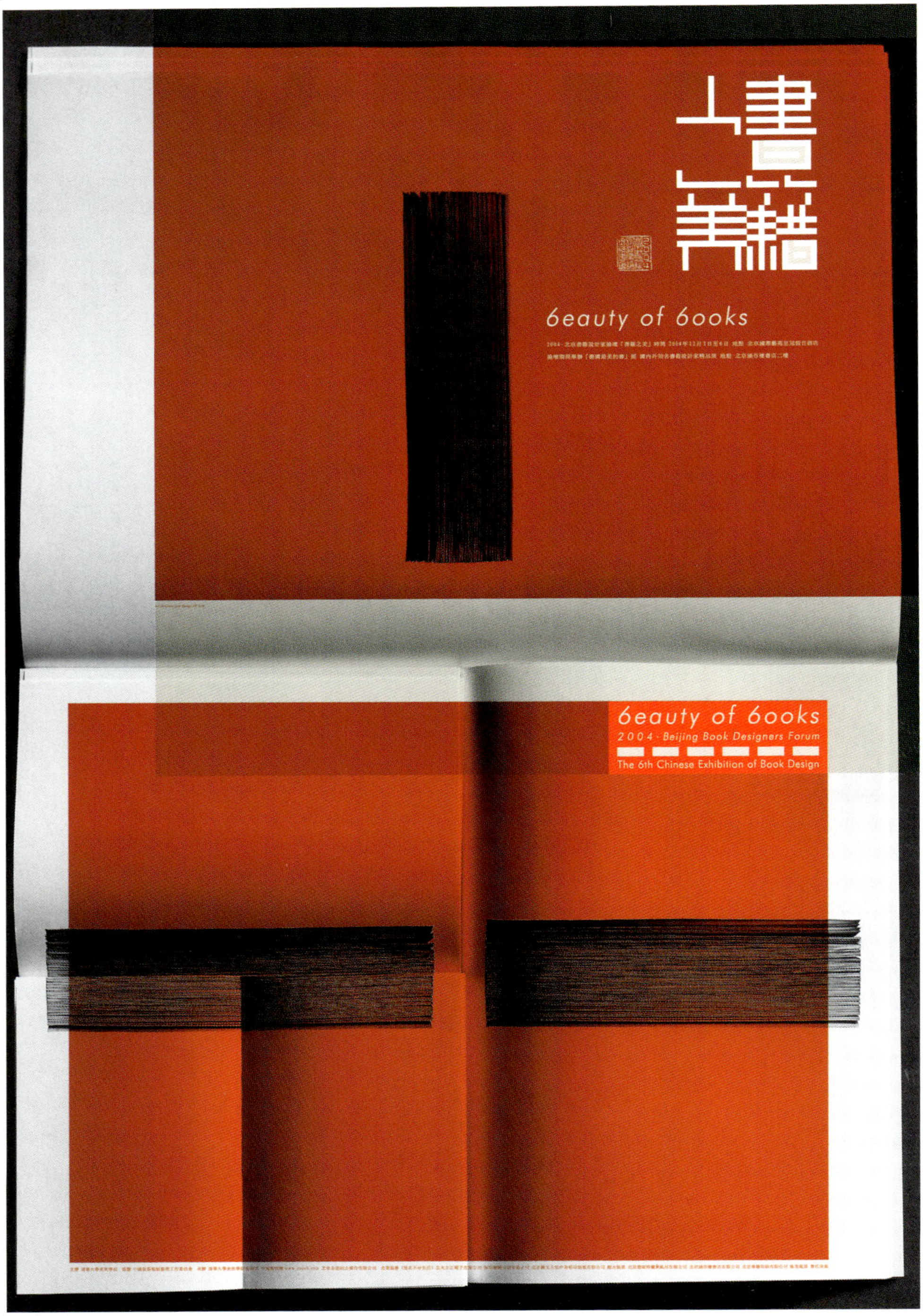

2 **He Jun**
Beauty of Books/6th Chinese Exhibition of Book Design
2005

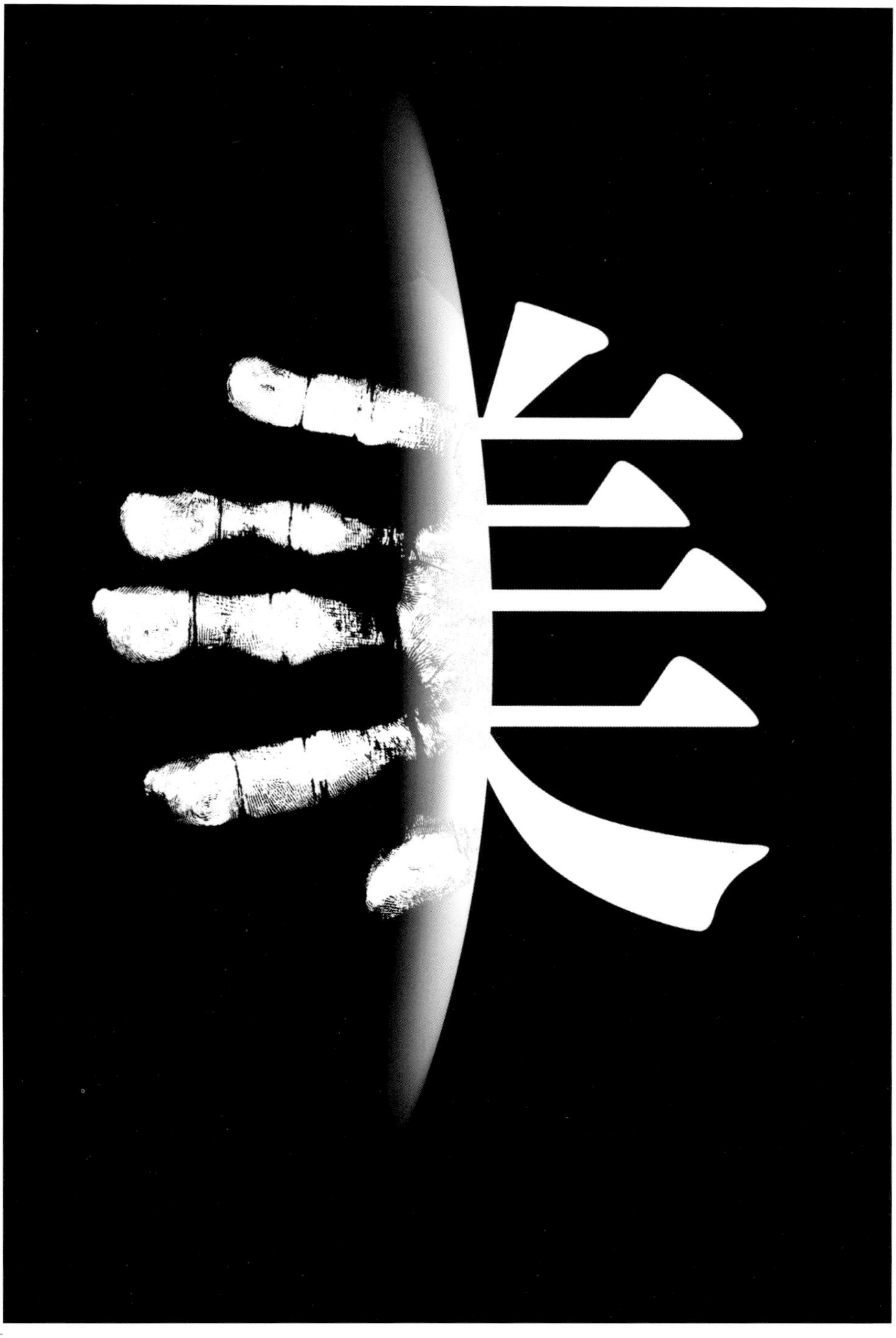

3 **Han Jiaying**
Frontiers
美 «schön» – “beautiful”
1997

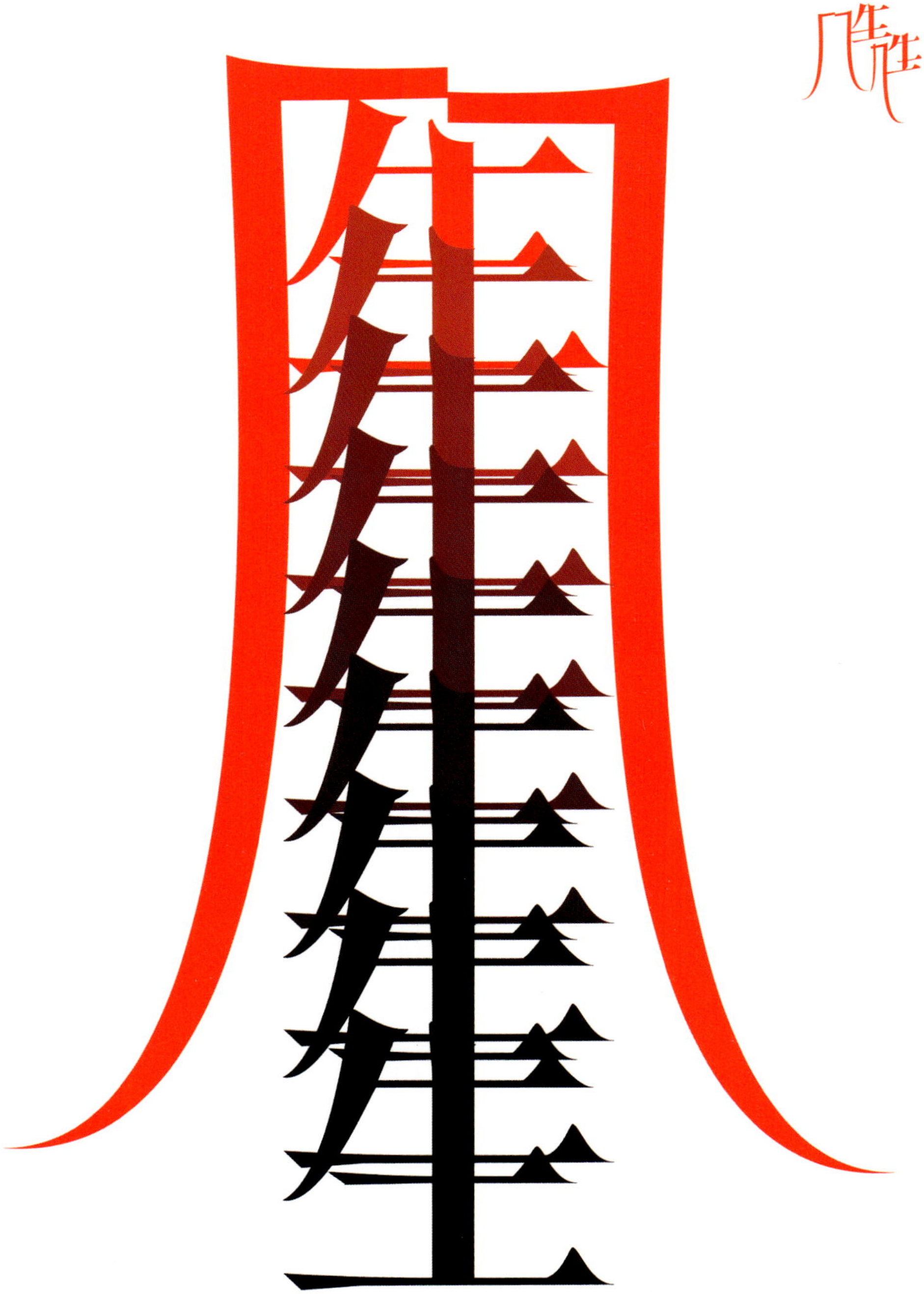

4 **Chen Guojin**
Neun Leben – Nine Lives
九生
2004

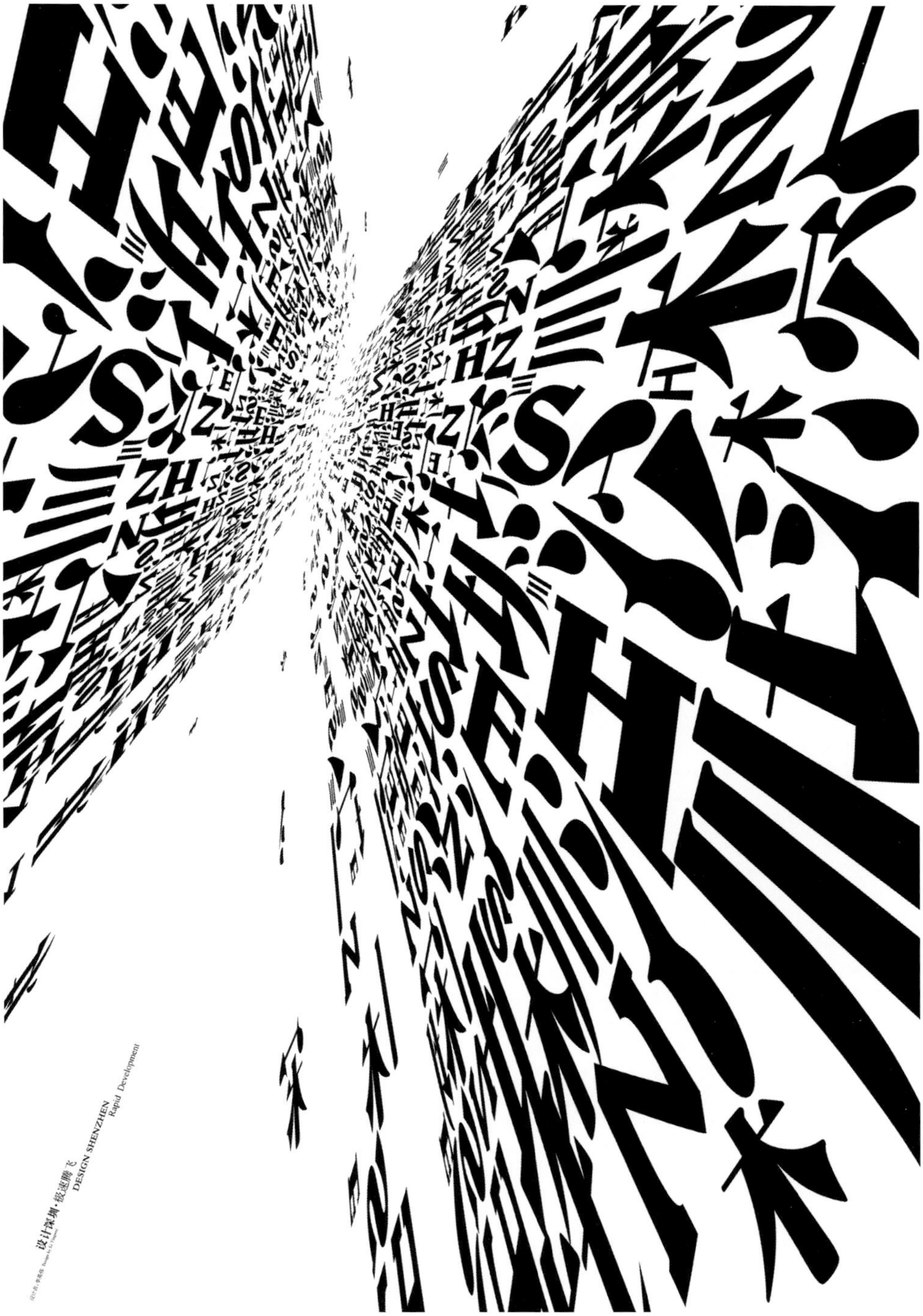

5 **Li Yingwei**
Design Shenzhen / Schnelle Entwicklung
– Rapid Development
2003

6 **Bob Chen**
Vier – Four
肆
2005

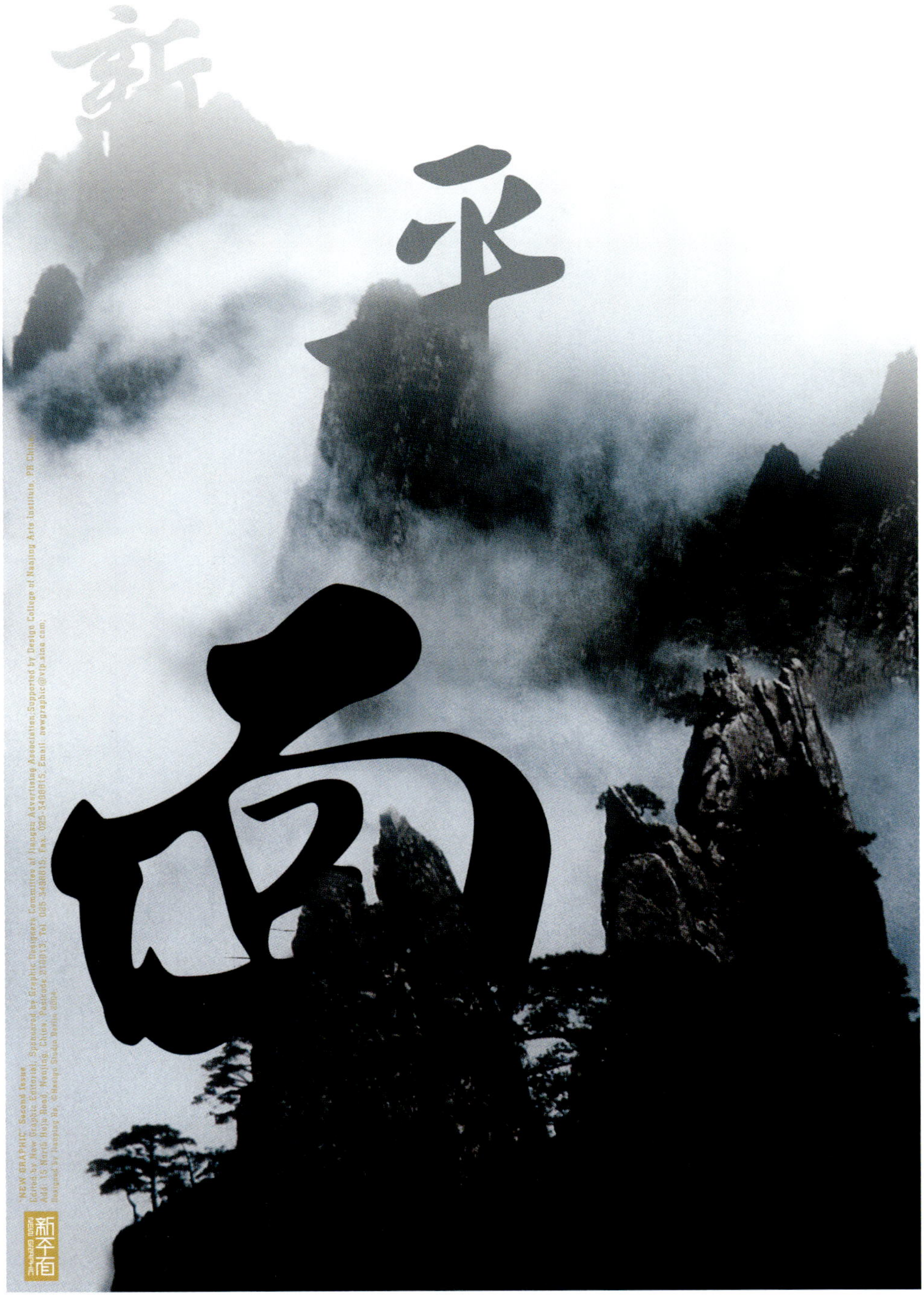

7 **He Jianping**
New Graphic
新平面
2003

Typo China

Eva Lüdi Kong

Schriftzeichen sind im chinesischen Stadtbild allgegenwärtig. Als Ladenaufschriften über ganzen Schaufensterreihen oder Neonlettern an Fassaden mehrstöckiger Restaurants zieren sie die Gebäude der Grossstädte, auf Megaprints von Werbeplakaten verdecken sie die letzten Ruinen der bescheidenen, niederen Ziegeldachhäuser, die noch vor zwei Jahrzehnten das Stadtbild bestimmt hatten. «Finde den individuellen Weg!», fordert in kraftvoll voranstrebendem Schriftzug das Werbeplakat einer Kleidermarke. «Arbeiten wir gemeinsam am Aufbau des Vaterlandes!», ist auf der Ummauerung der Baustelle eines neuen Wohnblockviertels in kahler Druckschrift zu lesen. Und hoch oben auf dem Dach eines eben erst aus dem Boden geschossenen Hochhauses werben selbstsicher vier Meter hohe Zeichenriesen mit den Worten: «Die Zukunft liegt in meiner Hand.»

Das neue Selbstbewusstsein, das mit dem wirtschaftlichen Erfolg des riesigen Landes einhergeht, ist der Boden, auf dem die jungen Grafikerinnen und Grafiker Chinas mehr und mehr ihre eigenen Ideen verwirklichen. Immer leichter verstehen sie auch mit der Vielfalt der Massstäbe und Werte umzugehen, die hier ineinander verwoben sind und in deren Spannungsfeld die Menschen denken und fühlen: das Traditionelle und das Neue; der von westlichen Werten angespornte Individualismus und die fest verwurzelten Gedanken des Zusammenhaltes innerhalb von Staat und Familie; die in Visionen einer schönen Zukunft umgewandelten verblassten Ideale des Sozialismus und die heile Welten vorgaukelnden Konsumversprechen der nunmehr alles durchdringenden Marktwirtschaft.

Ein Blick in die jüngste Vergangenheit zeigt, wie jung die neue chinesische Plakatgrafik tatsächlich ist – einmal abgesehen von den Anfängen kommerzieller Werbeplakate im kolonialen Shanghai der 1920er Jahre und deren Ablösung durch staatliche Propagandaplakate während der drei Jahrzehnte nach der Gründung der Volksrepublik im Jahr 1949. Das Fach Grafik-Design existiert an chinesischen Akademien und Hochschulen erst seit Mitte der 1980er Jahre. Doch auch da spielte es noch jahrelang eine untergeordnete Rolle als Teilbereich der «dekorativen Künste», die mit weniger hohen Prüfungshürden belegt waren als die Fächer der bildenden Kunst wie Ölmalerei, Skulptur oder traditionelle Tuschemalerei. Es war in jenen angesehenen Kunstfächern, wo damals angehende Künstler begannen, den staatlich festgelegten Einheitsstil der inhaltsbetonten realistischen Malerei zu durchbrechen, Scheinheiligkeiten offen zu legen und persönliche Haltungen einzunehmen. Im Verlauf der 1990er Jahre jedoch, als durch die Politik der Öffnung die städtischen Zentren zusehends kommerzialisiert wurden und die neue Konsumwelt über die Menschen hereinbrach, traten solche Werte in den Hintergrund. Auf einmal schien das Glück käuflich, und das Geld drohte zum wichtigsten Wertmassstab zu werden. Die Werbebranche verlangte dringend ausgebildete Grafiker, und das Fach Grafik-Design, das nun lukrative Aussichten versprach, bekam enormen Zulauf. Nachdem künstlerische Ansprüche jahrzehntelang von einer ideologisch geprägten Ästhetik bestimmt waren, stellte die reflektierte Beschäftigung mit der Plakatgestaltung nun eine Herausforderung dar. Erste Orientierungshilfen boten Plakate aus Hongkong und Taiwan. Hier war Grafik-Design bereits in den 1960er Jahren gefördert und von ausländischen Einflüssen geprägt worden. In diesen kapitalistischen Zentren der chinesischen Kultur, die von der traditionsfeindlichen Kulturrevolution (1966–1976) unberührt geblieben waren, hatte sich die Werbebranche vor allem während des Wirtschaftswachstums der 1970er Jahre entwickelt. Solche Vorläufer, bald gefolgt von Beispielen aus europäischen Ländern, wurden nun in der Volksrepublik erst einmal ausgiebig kopiert – ganz nach dem Muster traditioneller chinesischer Didaktik, die dem Nachahmen der Meister grossen Wert beimisst. Auf diese Weise lernten die angehenden Gestalterinnen und Gestalter, sich schnell und wendig in einem Durcheinander neuer Massstäbe zu bewegen, internationale Trends aufzunehmen und gleichzeitig die Bedürfnisse des chinesischen Marktes zu verfolgen.

Das Tor zum internationalen Erfolg eröffneten die seit den 1990er Jahren sich mehrenden internationalen Plakat-Biennalen und Wettbewerbe für Grafik-Design. Die um Anerkennung ringenden jungen Grafiker reagierten mit feinem Gespür auf die Vorlieben der Jurys. So konnte mitunter gerade die Betonung der chinesischen Schrift ein Indiz dafür sein, dass hier Design für nicht chinesische Augen geschaffen worden war. In dieser Hinsicht kam der Opportunismus dieser Generation letztlich ihr selbst zugute – traditionelle Werte, die aus politischen Gründen über lange Zeit hinweg allzu stark vernachlässigt worden waren, fanden nicht zuletzt auf dem Umweg über den westlichen Blick wieder zu ihrem eigentlichen Wert. Inzwischen ist in China parallel zur «Globalisierung» genannten Verwestlichung eine Rückorientierung zu den Werten der eigenen Kultur zu beobachten: insbesondere zu den traditionellen Künsten sowie zu den Lebensphilosophien des Daoismus und Konfuzianismus.

Gefragt sind in der Volksrepublik Gestalter mit weit gefächerten Fähigkeiten, die von Corporate Design über Werbung bis zur Titelblattgestaltung alles anbieten. Die Nachfrage nach Plakaten beschränkt sich allerdings auf Werbeplakate – öffentliche Aufträge bilden die Ausnahme. Erst seit wenigen Jahren werden in geringem Umfang nicht kommerzielle Plakate, beispielsweise für kulturelle Anlässe, hergestellt. Unter diesen Umständen hat sich das Gestalten von Plakaten teilweise zu einer Art Freizeitbeschäftigung entwickelt. Grafiker und Künstler äussern sich oft zu selbst gewählten Themen und stellen die Ergebnisse nur im kleinen Kreis vor, beispielsweise auf den nationalen Grafik-Biennalen. Dies erklärt auch, weshalb der weitaus grösste Teil anspruchsvoller Plakate noch kaum den Weg in die Öffentlichkeit findet. Der Trend zur Typografie, der in Hongkong und Taiwan um rund ein Jahrzehnt früher zu konstatieren ist, tritt jedoch in den chinesischen Medien immer klarer in Erscheinung.

Insbesondere im Fernsehen wird die Zeichenschrift mehr und mehr als autonomes Gestaltungsmittel eingesetzt.

Die Schrift – in der traditionellen chinesischen Kalligrafie unter höchste künstlerische Ansprüche gestellt – war in der Volksrepublik über Jahrzehnte hinweg weitgehend zur Übermittlung ideologischer Botschaften degradiert. Zeitgenössische Künstler suchten in den späten 1980er Jahren eine neue Annäherung an die Schrift, indem sie etwa in absurdisierender Weise die grossformatigen Wandbeschriftungen der Kulturrevolution imitierten oder ganze Zeichensätze von inexistenten, unlesbaren Zeichen entwarfen. In den hier versammelten Plakaten erhält nun die Zeichenschrift unter neuen Gesichtspunkten Beachtung.

Im Gegensatz zur Alphabetschrift, deren Buchstaben eine rein lautliche Existenz pflegen und sich zu Worten und Zeilen formieren, beinhaltet das chinesische Schriftsystem eine reiche und hochinteressante semantische Kultur. Das einzelne Zeichen besitzt eine starke visuelle Ausdruckskraft und wirkt für den Aussenstehenden wie ein abstraktes Bild, dessen Elemente scheinbar ohne Anfang und Ende ineinander verschachtelt, übereinander geschichtet, nebeneinander gereiht sind. Jedes Schriftzeichen stellt eine bildhafte Aussage dar. Es ist im Grunde so zu lesen wie ein Gegenstand, den wir anschauen und gleichzeitig benennen; ja es IST nachgerade der Gegenstand.

Wer chinesische Zeichen lesen und schreiben lernt, begibt sich auf eine Reise entlang der Spuren längst vergangener Zeiten: Er lernt die Bilder von Sonne und Mond erkennen, die Bilder von Himmel und Erde, von Hand, Fuss, Auge und Mund. Mit jedem neuen Schriftbild erkennt der Lernende etwas mehr von dem komplexen Zusammenspiel inhaltlicher und phonetischer Elemente und der umfassenden Logik, die dem scheinbar spielerisch gewachsenen System der chinesischen Schrift innewohnt. Im Grunde wird in dieser Schrift die Welt eingeteilt: Alles, was flüssig und nass ist, wird mit dem Sinnträger «Wasser» versehen, beispielsweise 河 *hé* («Fluss»), 海 *hǎi* («Meer»), 汁 *zhī* («Saft»), 浴 *yù* («Bad»). Alles, was brennt oder kocht, wird mit «Feuer» gekennzeichnet, zum Beispiel 热 *rè* («heiss»), 焦 *jiāo* ("verkohlt"), 煮 *zhǔ* («kochen») ... Und immer wieder als Zeichenbestandteile: Kühe und Hunde, Pferde und Tiger, Fische und Vögel, Überbleibsel aus einer fernen Zeit, die stumm im chinesischen Alltag weiterleben und sich erstaunlich reibungslos in die moderne Welt einfügen.

In verschiedenen Arbeiten werden bestimmte Schriftzeichen auf ihre ursprüngliche, konkrete Botschaft zurückgeführt, wobei die Bildlichkeit oft in verfremdeter Weise dargestellt wird. So füllt beispielsweise Liu Zhizhi in *One-m² field* (54) die Leerstellen des Zeichens 田 *tián* («Feld») mit hellgrünen Grasflächen aus und schafft damit eine ungewohnte Negativansicht, die gleichzeitig die ursprüngliche bildliche Botschaft wiederherstellt. In ähnlicher Weise geht Stanley Wong (41, 43) vor, der piktografische Bestandteile von Zeichen durch fotografische Abbildungen mit gleicher Aussage ersetzt. Dadurch wird sowohl der Blick des Lesenden durch das allzu deutlich dargestellte Bild befremdet wie auch der Blick des Schauenden durch das übrig gebliebene Zeichenelement mit entstellter Aussage irritiert.

Dass Schrift und Bild einander ergänzen und ineinander übergehen, ist in China nichts Neues. Sowohl in der traditionellen Tuschemalerei wie auch in der volksnahen, illustrativen Holzschnittkunst war es durchaus üblich, dass die Bildfläche beschriftet wurde, sodass die Schrift ein inhärenter Bestandteil des Bildes war. Direkte Anlehnung an diese Tradition finden wir bei He Jianpings *New Graphic* (7), wo die Schriftzeichen als gegenständliche Elemente in die einer Tuschemalerei nachempfundene Landschaftsfotografie eingesetzt werden.

Die Beschäftigung mit der chinesischen Schrift führt unweigerlich auch zur traditionellen Kalligrafie, die in China als höchste Kunst geachtet wird. Hier ist weder dekorative noch ornamentale Bearbeitung gefragt, vielmehr geht es um die Ausdruckskraft der spannungsvoll bewegten und belebten Linien sowie um ein vielfältiges und harmonisches Zusammenspiel von Schwarz und Weiss. Jiang Hua beschreibt die Kalligrafie als Knotenpunkt der chinesischen Kunst und Schlüssel zum Grafik-Design. Auch andere Grafiker berufen sich bei ihren Entwürfen auf dieses traditionelle Medium und benutzen mitunter die mit Pinsel geschriebenen schwarzen Schriftzeichen direkt als Ausdrucksmittel.

Eindrucksvoll sind die zwei Arbeiten *60th Anniversary of Atomic Bombing* von Wang Xu (49), der mit je zwei grossen Schriftzeichen, schwarz auf weiss, Plakate von höchster Ausdruckskraft geschaffen hat, deren Botschaft sowohl für Lesende wie auch für Schriftunkundige unmittelbar sinnlich erfassbar ist.

Im chinesischen Kulturraum spielt die Schrift als kulturtragendes Element eine wichtige Rolle. Nicht nur ihr Bilderreichtum, sondern auch die verschiedenen Stile und Erscheinungsformen rufen beim chinesischen Betrachter unmittelbar Assoziationen an kulturelle Zusammenhänge hervor. Ein Beispiel dieser Art ist das Plakat zum Thema Kommunikation von Chen Shaohua (51). Mit einfachen Mitteln werden hier reiche Assoziationsfelder geschaffen. Die in Schwarz und Weiss aufgeteilte Bildfläche evoziert die universale Polarität von Yin und Yang, visuell erkennbar als Licht und Dunkel oder als Himmel und Erde. In der Mitte liegen zwei Versionen des Zeichens *gōu* für «Wassergraben», das im Sinne eines freien Informationsflusses Teil des Wortes «Kommunikation» bildet. Oben erscheint es als traditionelles Langzeichen 溝, unten in der vereinfachten Form 沟, die seit den 1950er Jahren in der Volksrepublik üblich ist. Der beiden Zeichen gleich bleibende Bestandteil für «Wasser» formt das kleine visuelle Feld, in dem Kommunikation gerade zu geschehen scheint, wo weiss und schwarz sichtbar ineinander übergehen, während die anliegenden Zeichenteile bereits in der Mischfarbe Grau erscheinen. Zusätzlich zur Symbolik von Yin/Yang und klassisch/modern versucht Chen, indem er die Buchstaben des englischen Wortes «communication» mit den entsprechenden chinesischen Zeichen 沟通 *gōu tōng* verbindet, auch eine Kommunikation zwischen Ost und West herzustellen.

Trotz der Bedeutsamkeit der chinesischen Schrifttradition berufen sich längst nicht alle Gestalterinnen und Gestalter auf die Entwicklungsgeschichte der Zeichenschrift. Viele bevorzugen eine Annäherung an die Erscheinungsformen der Druckschrift, wie sie in den Fonts der Computer festgelegt ist. Hierbei wird oft ein eher von der westlichen Typografie geprägter Umgang mit der Schrift gepflegt – wie etwa das Ertasten der minimalen Lesbarkeit, wenn die Schriftzeichen beispielsweise nur halb erscheinen, wenn deren Striche auseinander fallen oder wenn konsequent jeder horizontale Strich weggelassen wird (46–48). Ein schönes Beispiel ist das im Auftrag einer Papierfirma gefertigte Plakat *Four* von Bob Chen (6), auf dem das Schriftzeichen des Wortes «vier» wie ein unbeschriebenes Blatt Papier als grosse weisse Fläche erscheint. Anhand der Konturen, die die komplexe Struktur des Zeichens hervorrufen, bleibt das Schriftzeichen problemlos lesbar.

Auch die lateinische Buchstabenschrift – in China dank der amtlichen Lautumschrift Pinyin und der Unumgänglichkeit der englischen Sprache allgemein verbreitet – bildet mitunter Gegenstand der grafischen Arbeiten. Vor dem Hintergrund der Zeichenschrift werden Buchstaben im Allgemeinen als eine Art entseelte Zeichen wahrgenommen: als abstrakte, rein lautliche Gebilde, die mangels adäquatem piktoralem Gehalt in der Lautumschrift kein chinesisches Schriftzeichen ausreichend zu umschreiben vermögen.

Insgesamt begegnen wir in den vorliegenden Plakaten äusserst reichhaltigen Formen des grafischen Umgangs mit der Schrift. Mitunter scheint es, als wäre unter den allzu schnell erweiterten Massstäben alles möglich geworden, als wäre alles gleichzeitig vorhanden.
Zurzeit befindet sich die visuelle Kultur Chinas in einer besonderen Phase der Entwicklung, in der sich hoffnungsvolle Perspektiven öffnen. Dennoch beklagen Fachleute Unzulänglichkeiten im chinesischen Grafik-Design, besonders was das Niveau in der täglichen Anwendung betrifft. Wang Xu etwa bezeichnet die allgegenwärtigen Kreationen für den Geschmack der grossen Masse als «Fastfood-Stil». Er bedauert, dass der Anteil anspruchsvoller Gestaltung zu gering ist und dass gute Arbeiten kaum wahrgenommen werden. Kritisiert wird zudem das weiterhin verbreitete unreflektierte Kopieren westlicher Vorlagen, das oft einhergeht mit der oberflächlichen Ausbeutung traditioneller Elemente. Gleichzeitig wird auf einen Mangel an qualifizierten Lehrkräften in der Ausbildung hingewiesen.

Ein Lichtblick bleibt für viele Gestalterinnen und Gestalter die Auseinandersetzung mit der Tradition. In der Rückbesinnung liegt ein Teil der Hoffnung, nach einer Zeit einseitig erlebter Beeinflussung durch westliche Massstäbe endlich im internationalen Rahmen eigenständige Ideen präsentieren zu können. Zu wünschen ist zudem, dass sich in der Volksrepublik eine reale Auftragskultur für anspruchsvolles Design etabliert.

Die unter dem Titel *Typo China* vorgestellten Schriftplakate bleiben für westliche Betrachter in mancher Hinsicht rätselhaft und verschlüsselt. Und doch ist es gerade die chinesische Zeichenschrift, deren Bildhaftigkeit und Ausdrucksstärke sowohl das Lesen wie auch das reine Betrachten der Plakate zu einem faszinierenden Erlebnis macht – ein Ertasten einer noch zu unbekannten kulturellen Atmosphäre, die uns weit über den grafisch-visuellen Bereich hinaus bereichern kann.

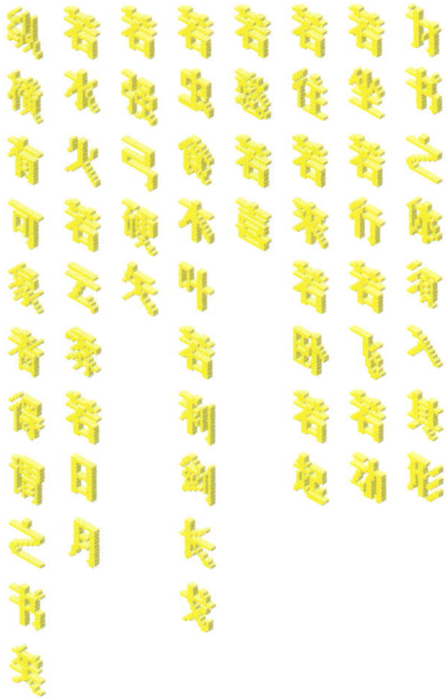

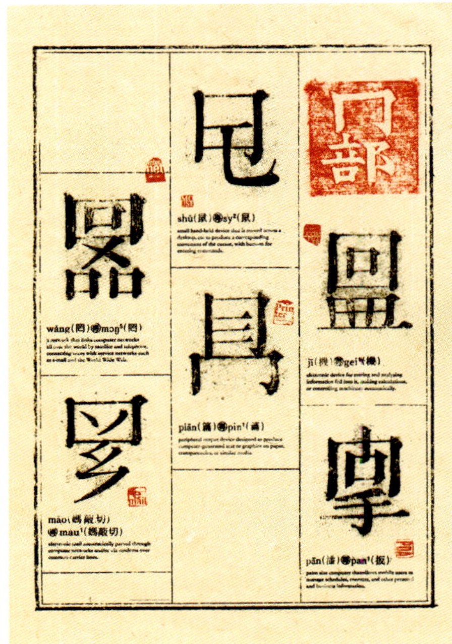

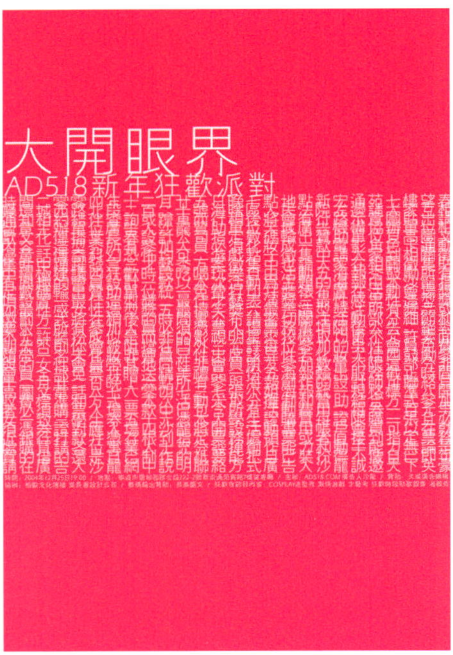

8 **Zhang Wanbao**
3D Font
2003

9 **Ye Changchun**
AD 518 New Year's Carnival/Qinghua University
2004

10 **Lam Hung**
Chinese Character
2003

11 **Lam Hung**
Peace of Mind – Zenter
心 «Herz» – "Heart", 2001

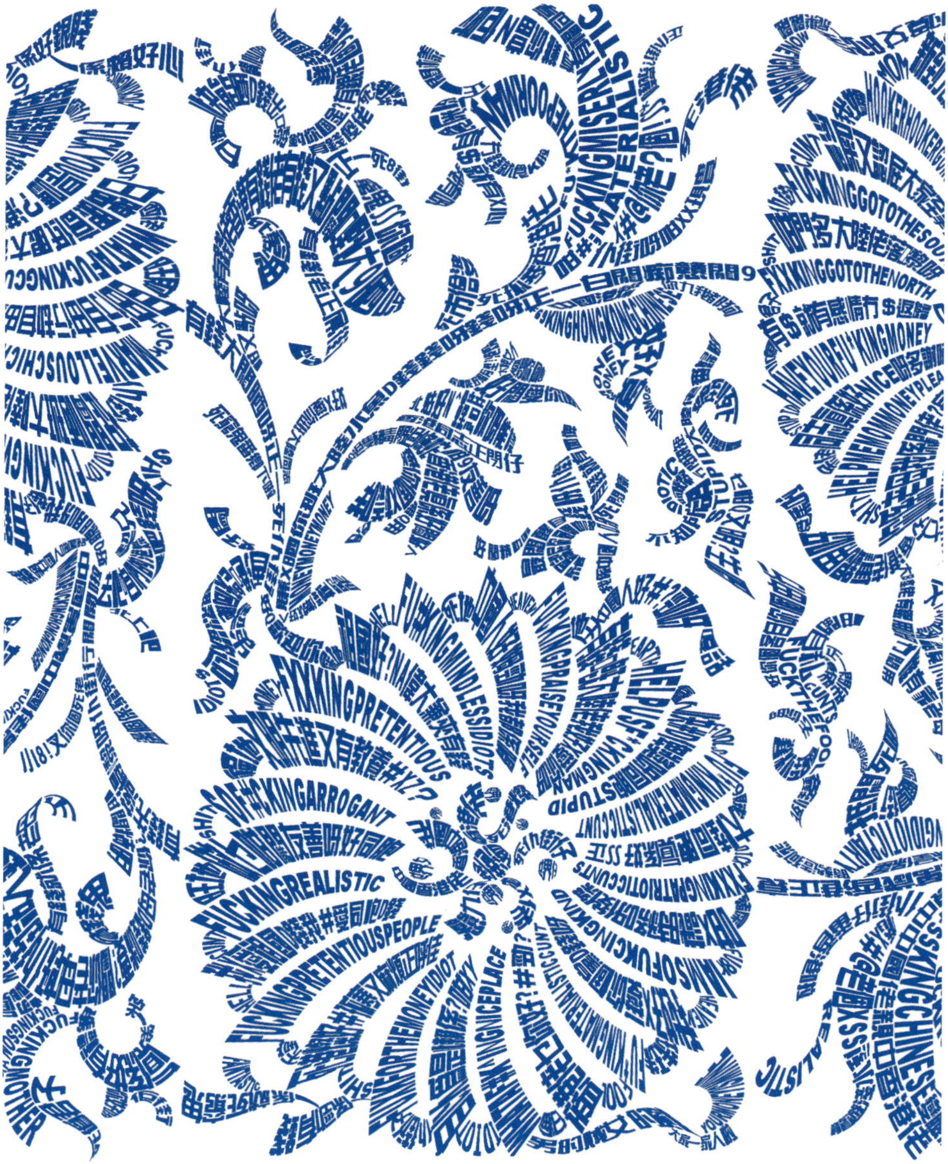

12 **Tsang Kin-wah**
Untitled
2004

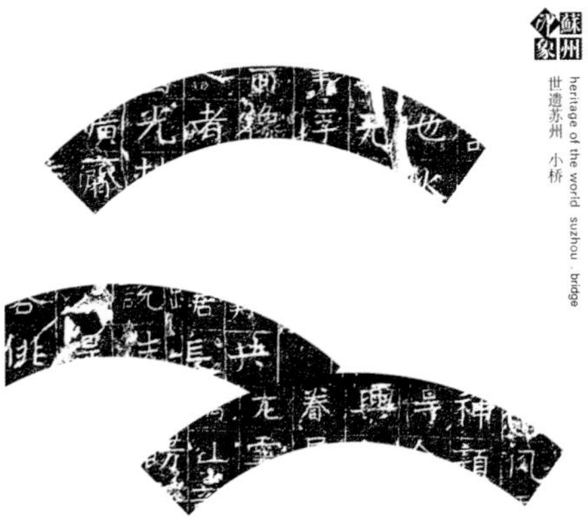

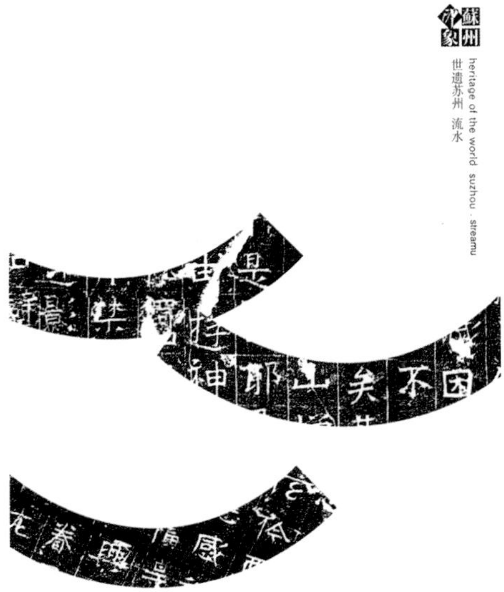

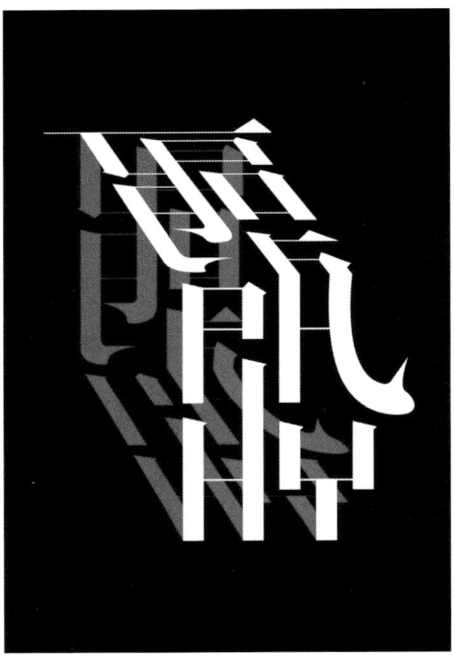

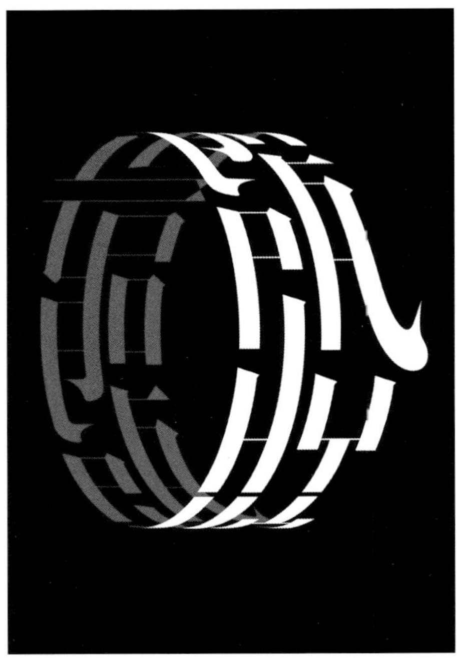

13 **Bai Zhiwei**
Welterbe Suzhou/Brücke –
Heritage of the World Suzhou/Bridge
2004

14/16 **Zhao Qing**
Typography, 2005

15 **Bai Zhiwei**
Welterbe Suzhou/Fluss –
Heritage of the World Suzhou/Stream
2004

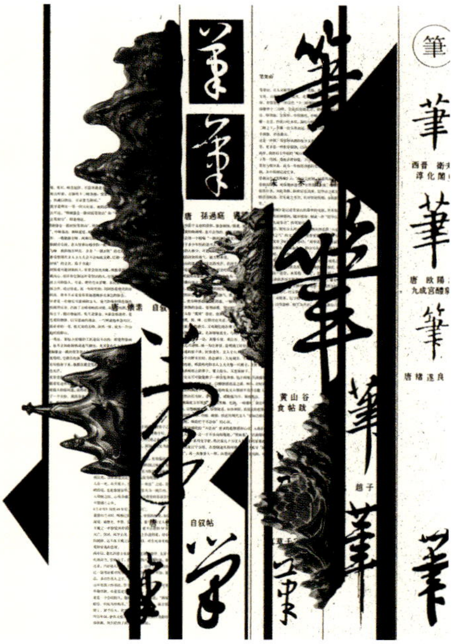

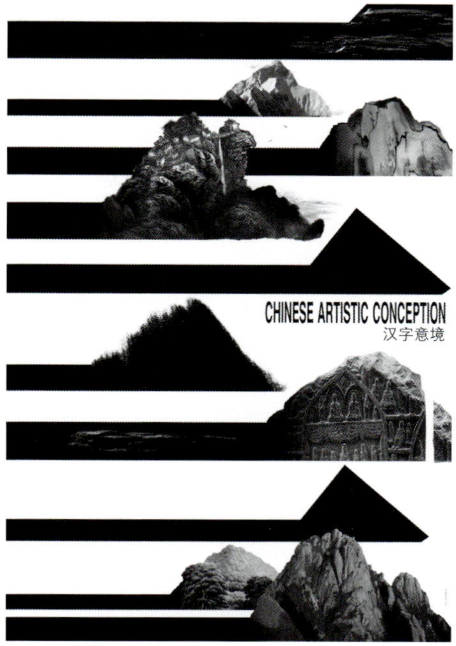

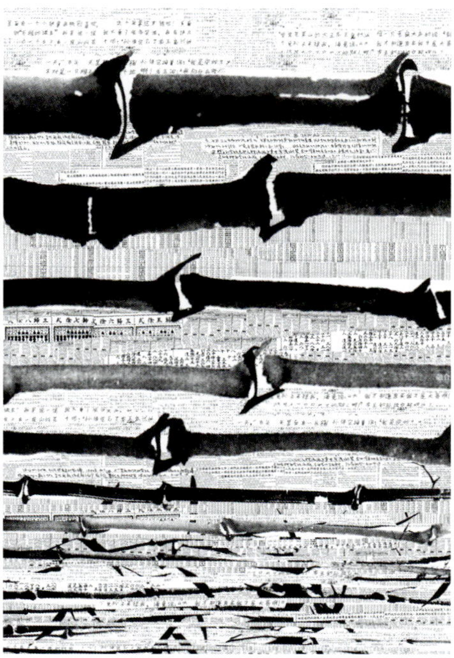

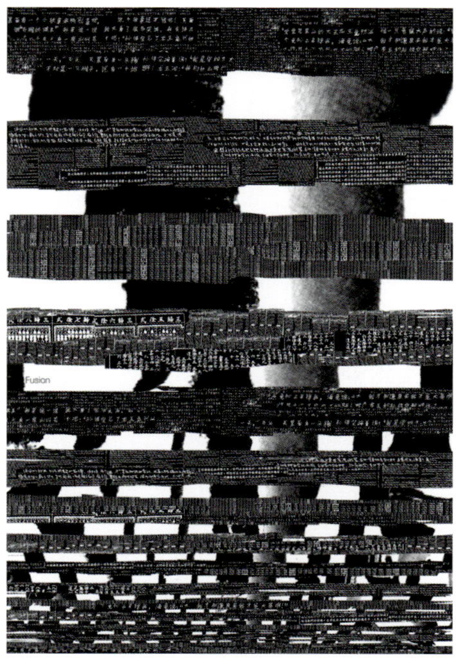

17 **Chen Yuanchuan**
Pinsel / Pinselhalter – Brush / rack
筆
2000

18/20 **Han Jiaying**
Fusion, 1999

19 **Chen Yuanchuan**
Chinese Artistic Conception
2000

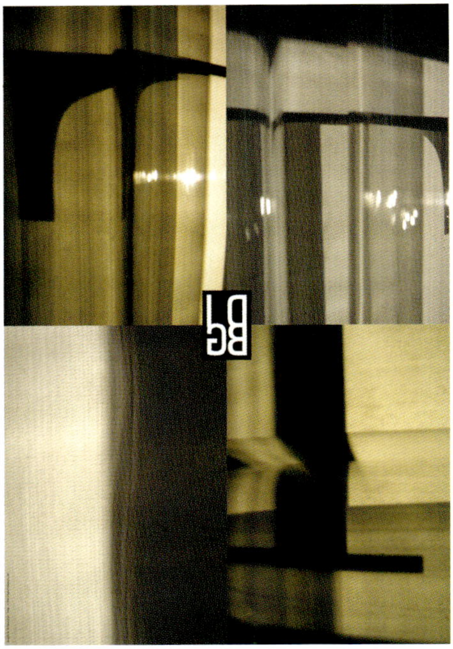

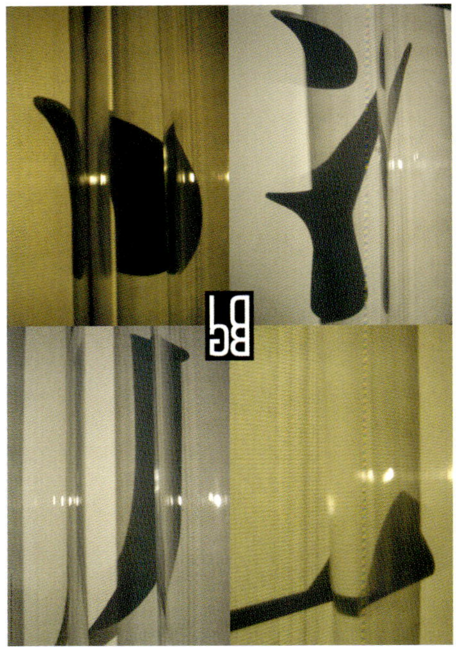

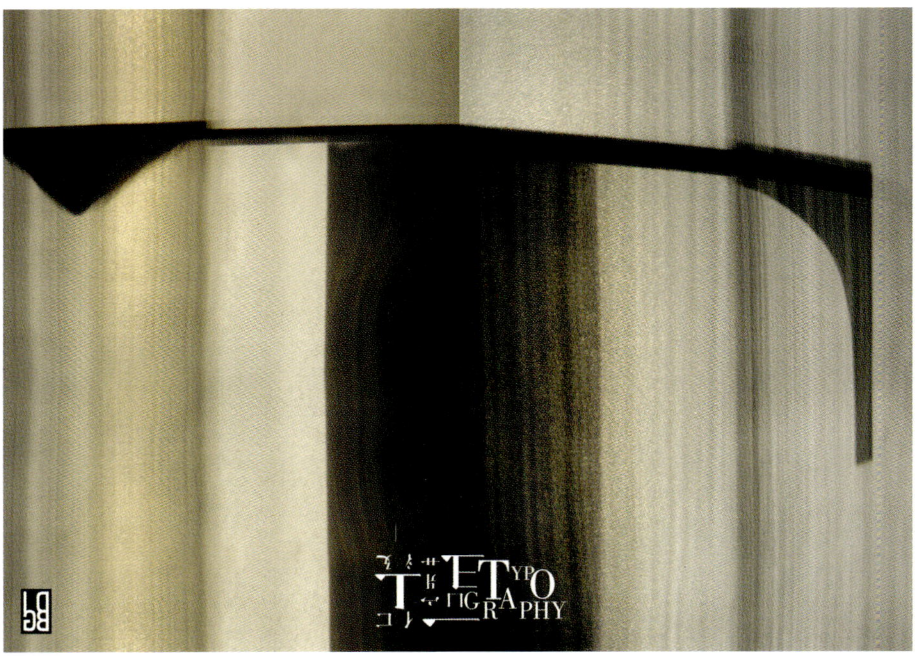

21–23 **Bi Xuefeng**
Typography
2004

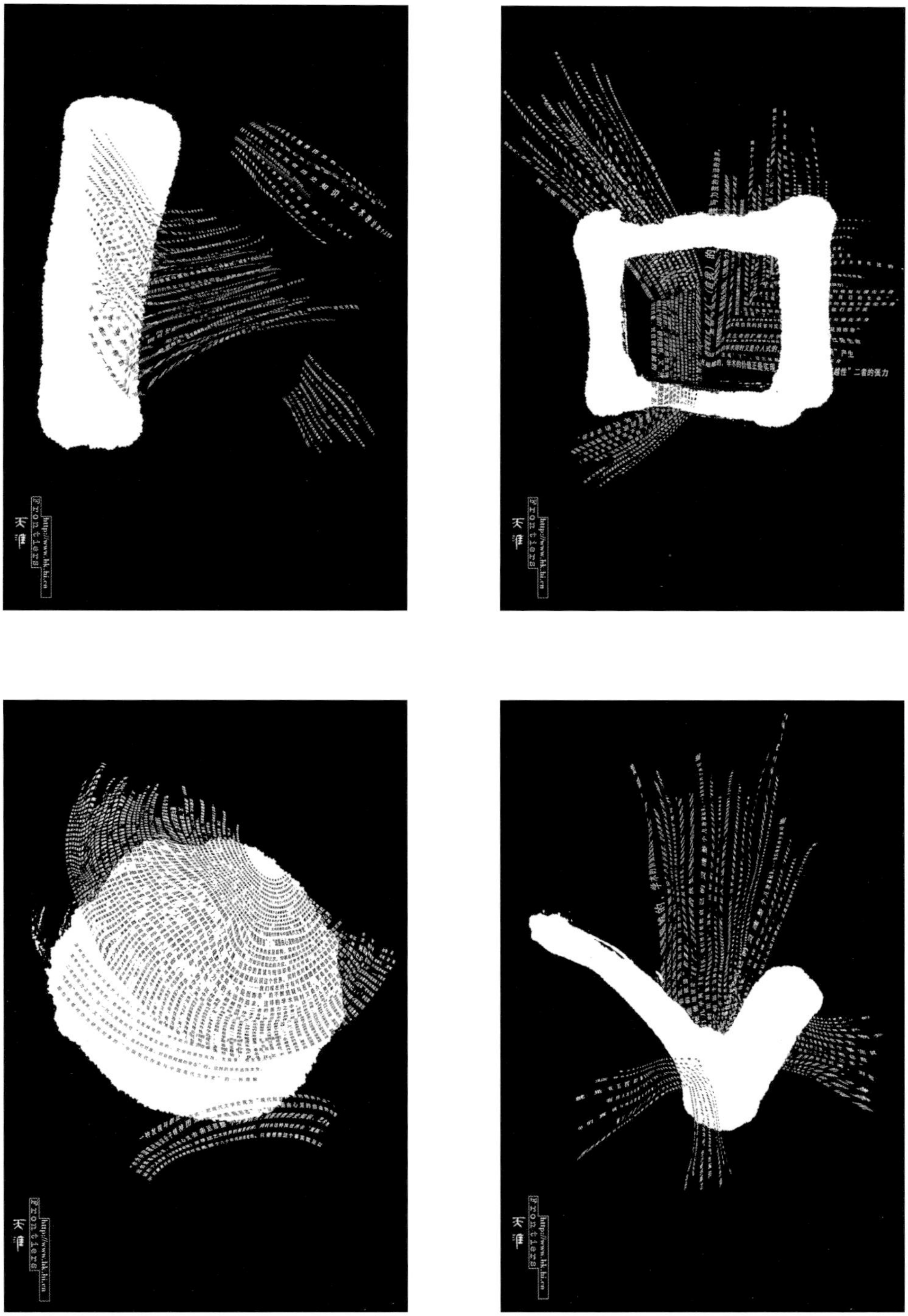

24–27 **Han Jiaying**
Frontiers
1999

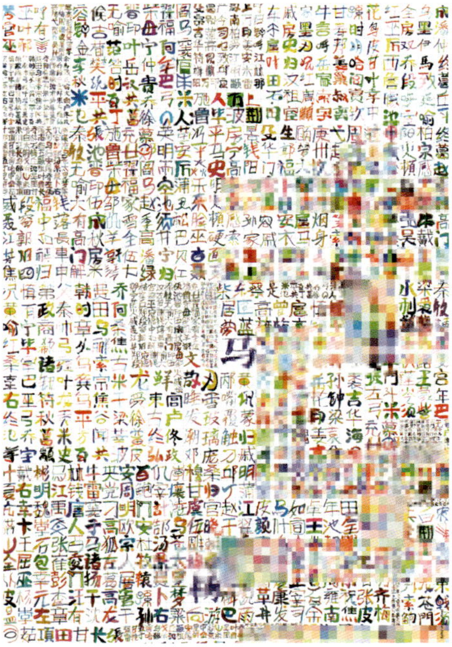

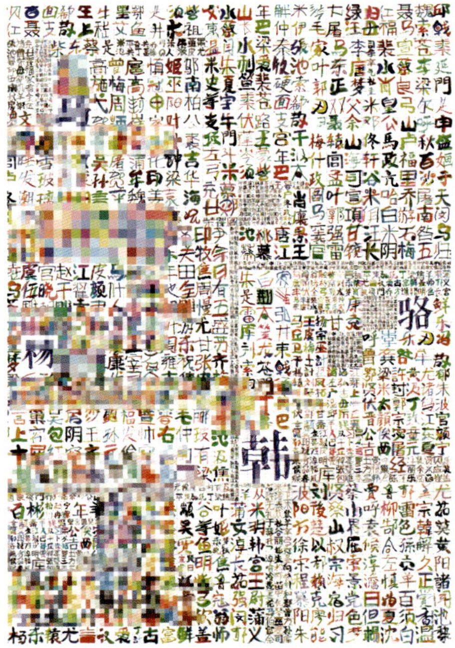

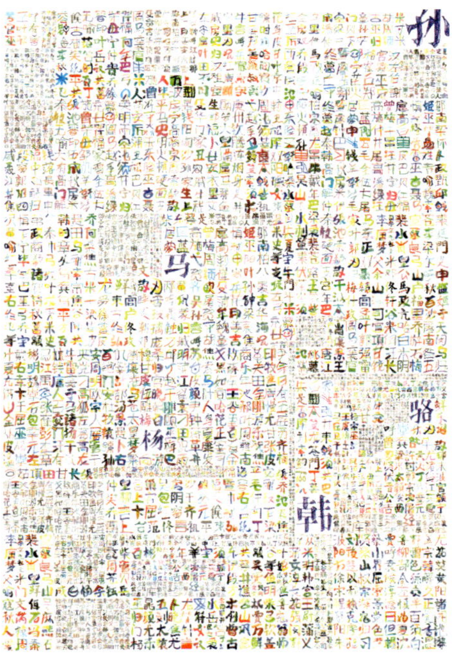

28–32 **Han Jiaying**
In China
2005

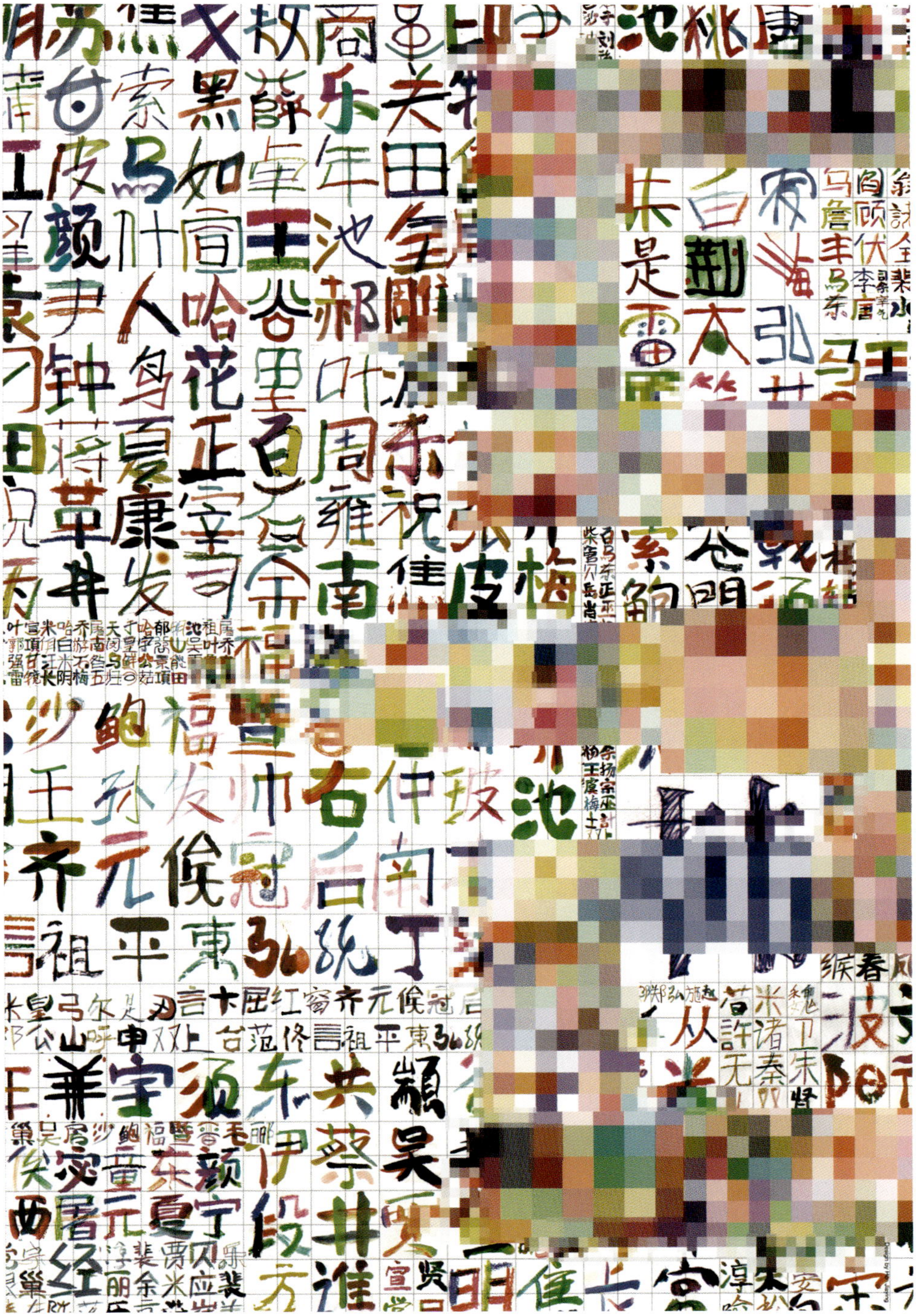

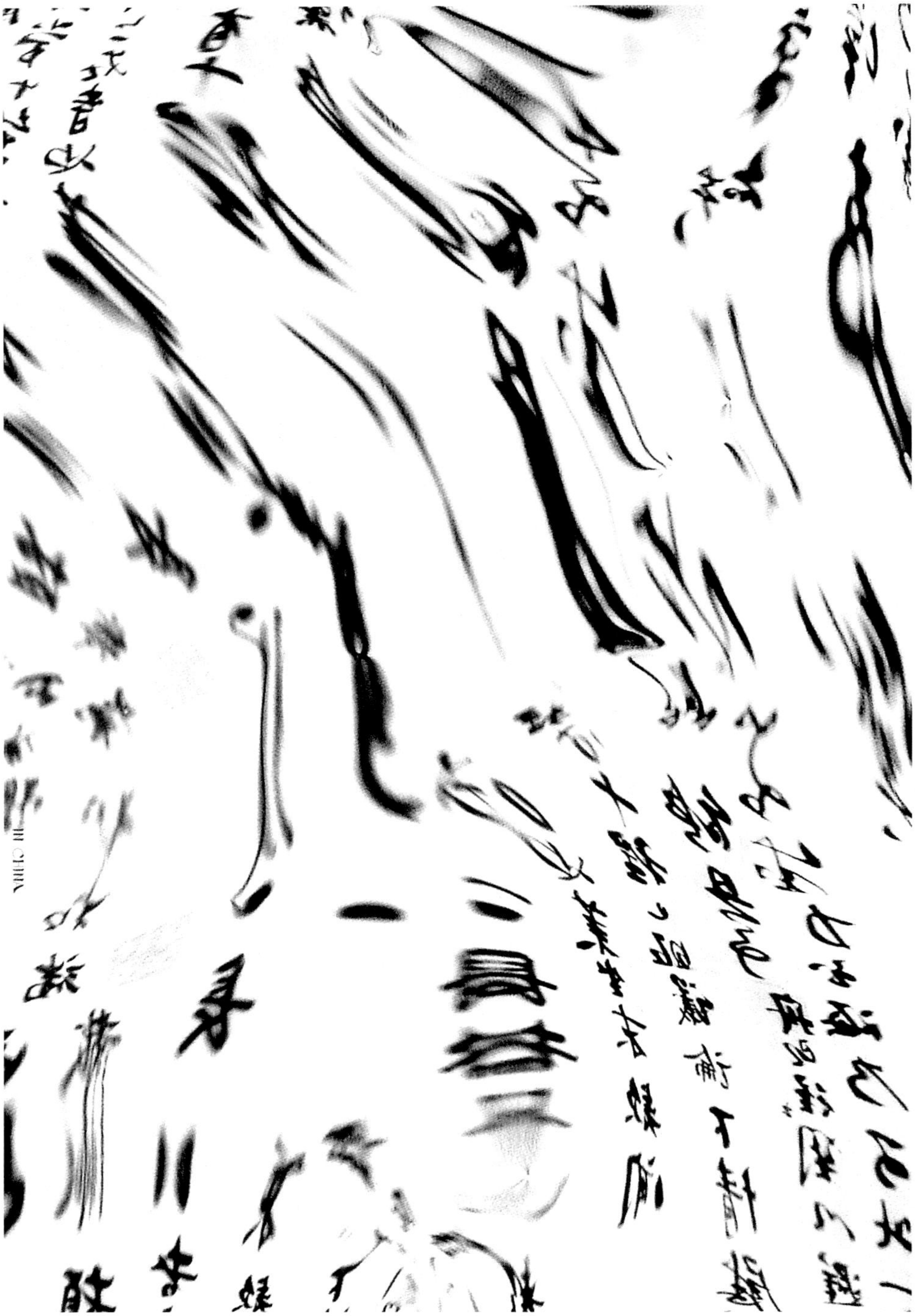

33 **Li Yingwei**
In China
2005

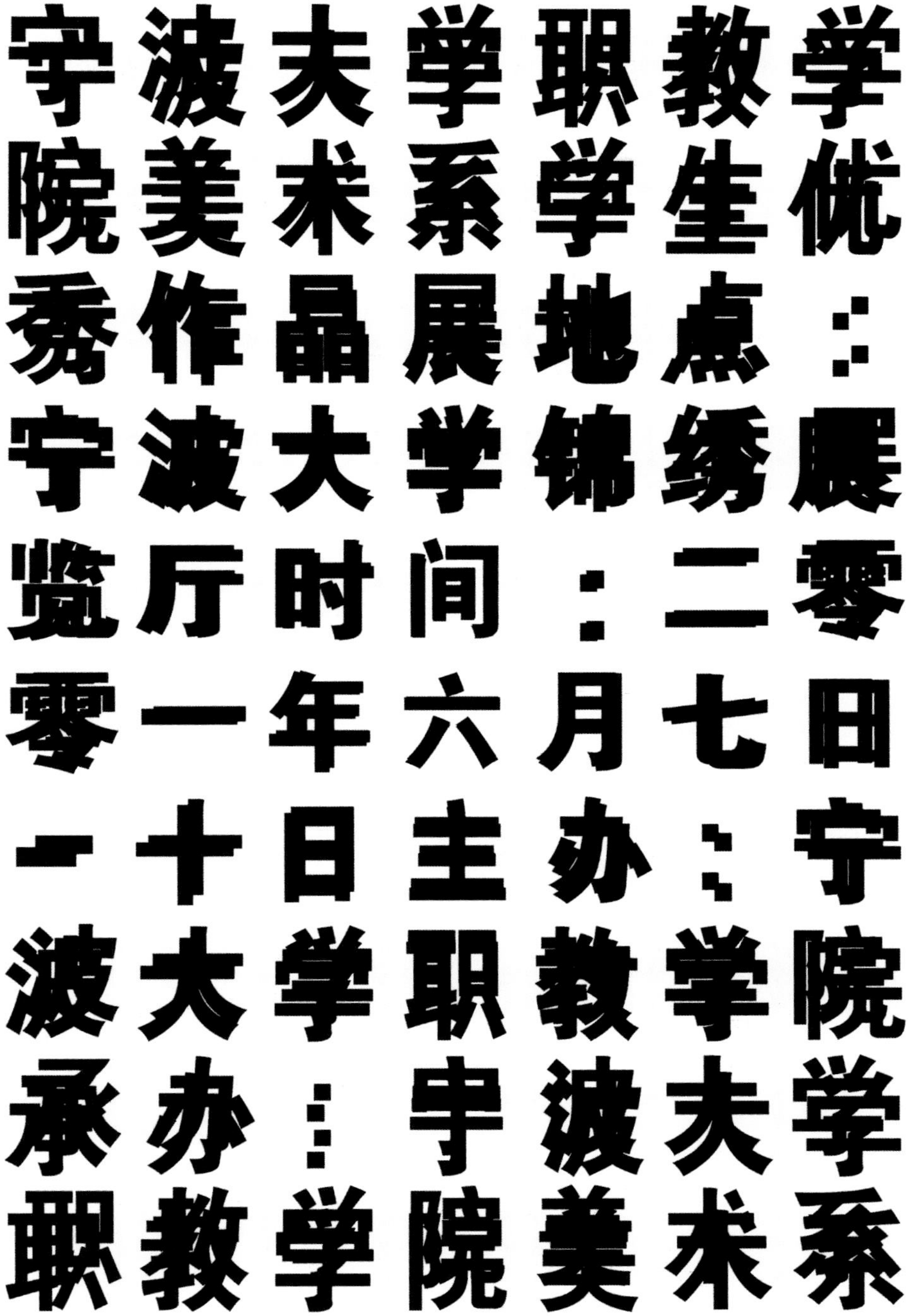

34 **Pan Qin**
The Exhibition of Exceptional Student Work/Ningbo University
2003

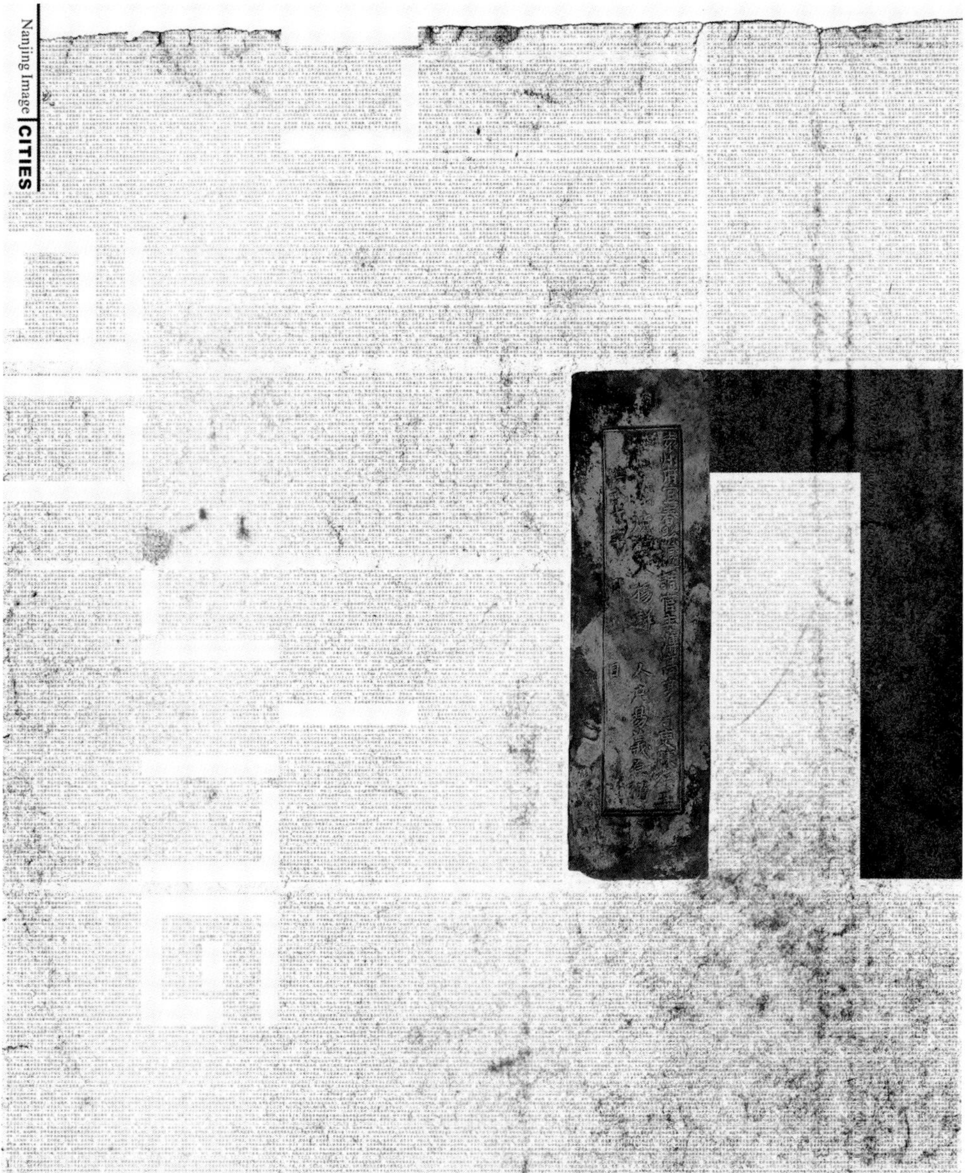

35 **Zhao Qing**
Nanjing Image Cities
2005

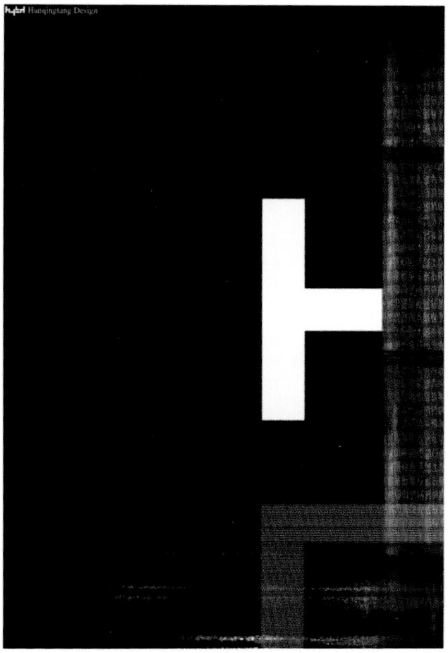

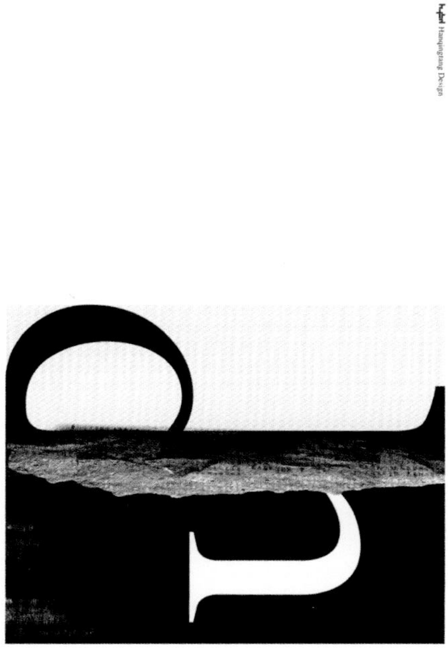

36–39 **Zhao Qing**
Hanqingtang Design
2005

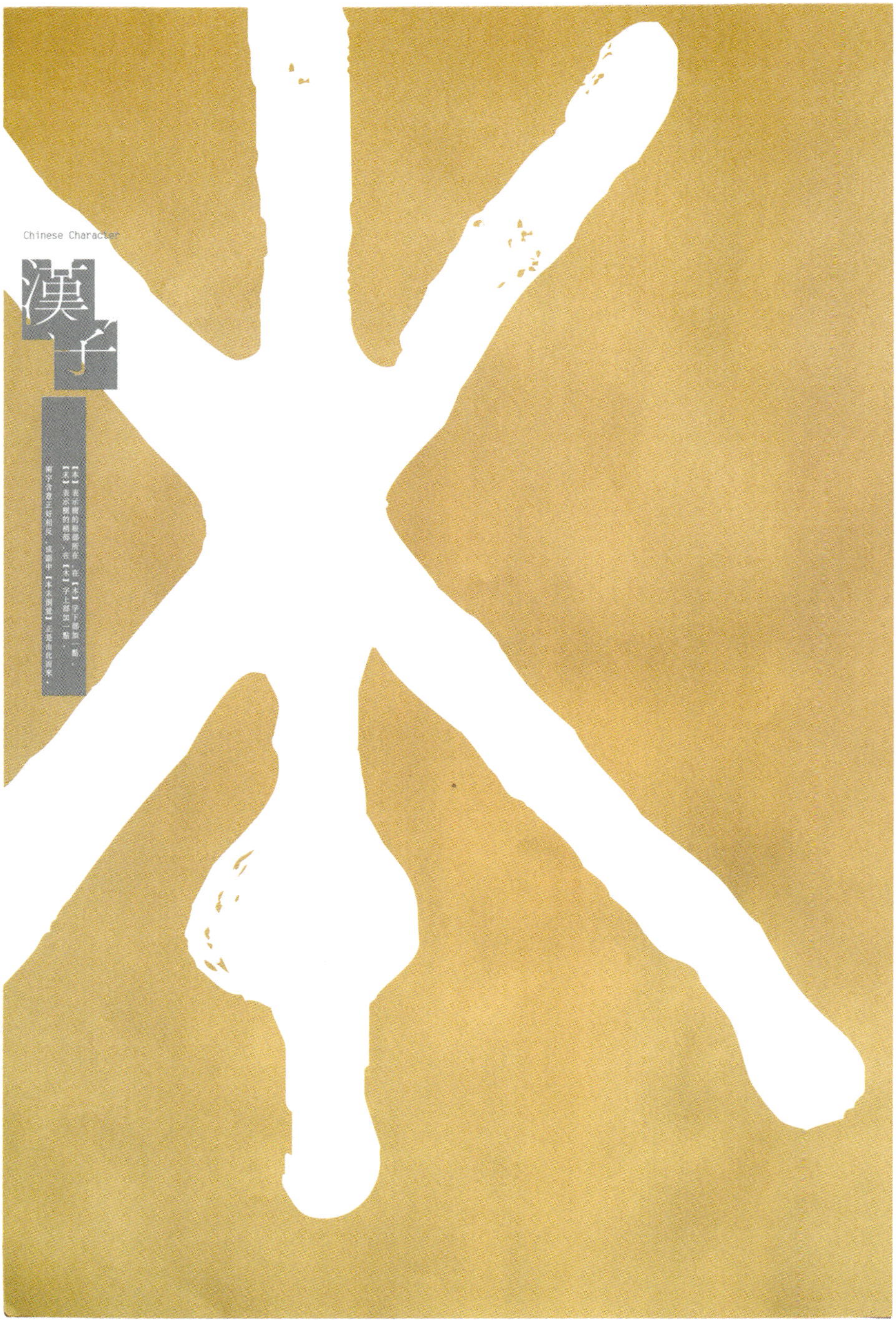

40 **Wang Yuefei**
“Take the branch for the Root”
本 «Ursprung» – “origin”
末 «Ende» – “end”
木 «Holz» – “wood”
2005

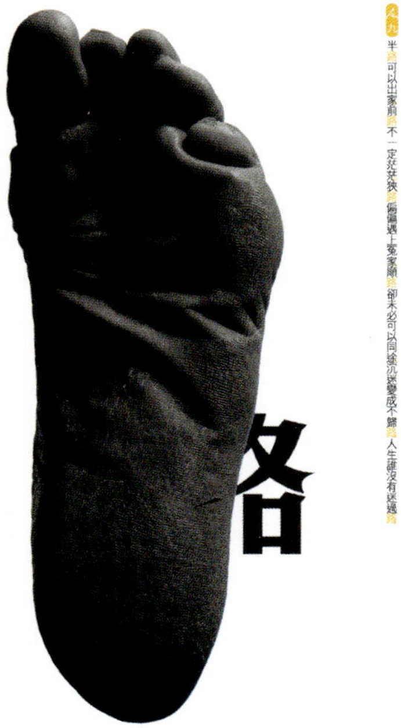

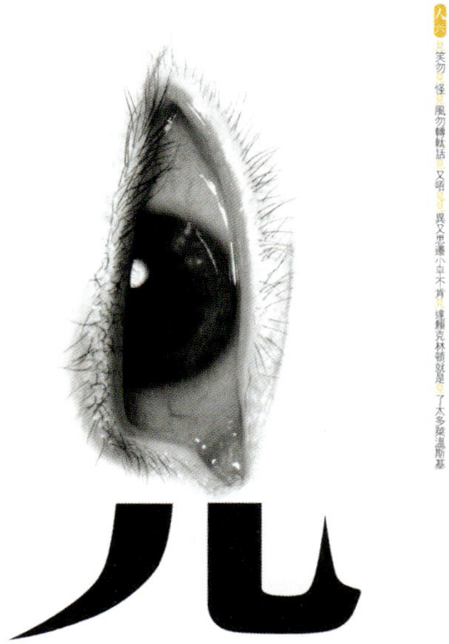

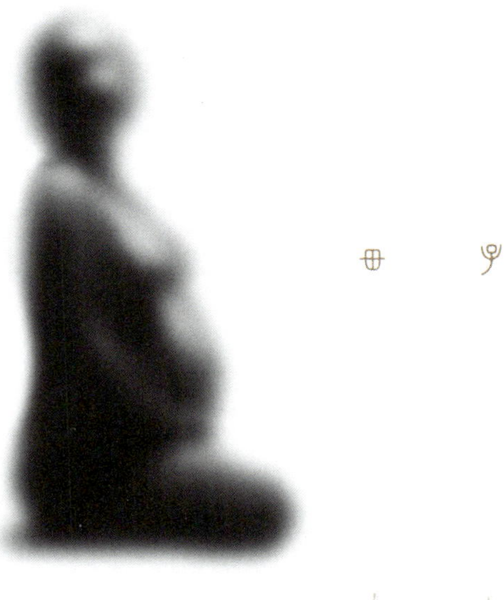

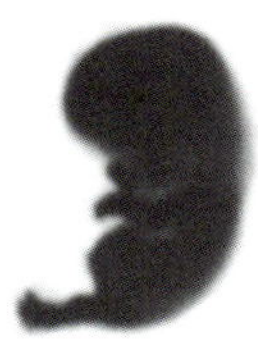

41 **Stanley Wong**
Fuss – Foot
路 «Weg» – "path", 2003

42 **Wong Imaya**
Mutter und Kind – Mother and child
母 «Mutter» – "mother", 2005

43 **Stanley Wong**
Auge – Eye
見 «sehen» – "to see", 2003

44 **Wong Imaya**
Mutter und Kind – Mother and child
子 «Kind» – "child", 2005

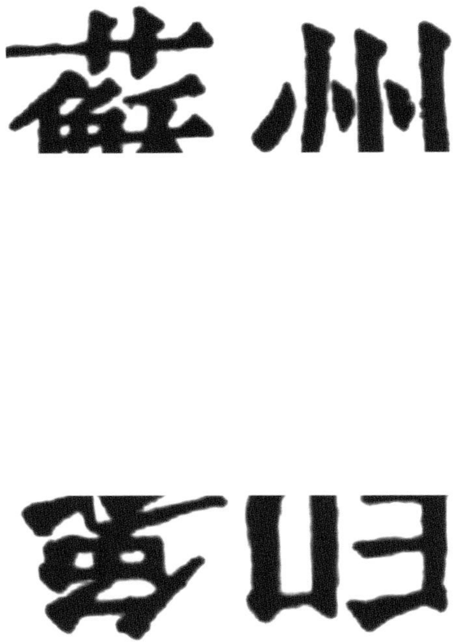

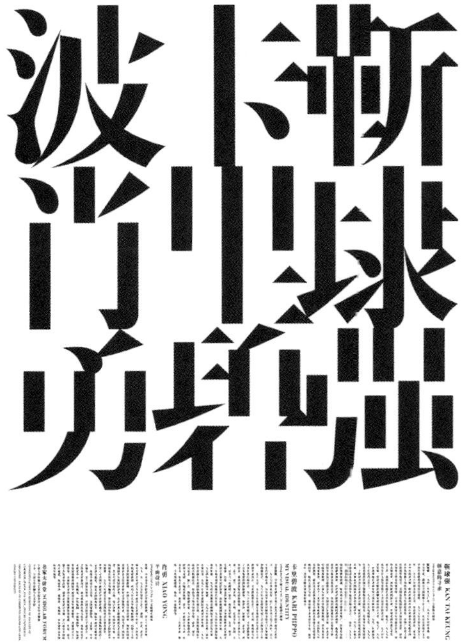

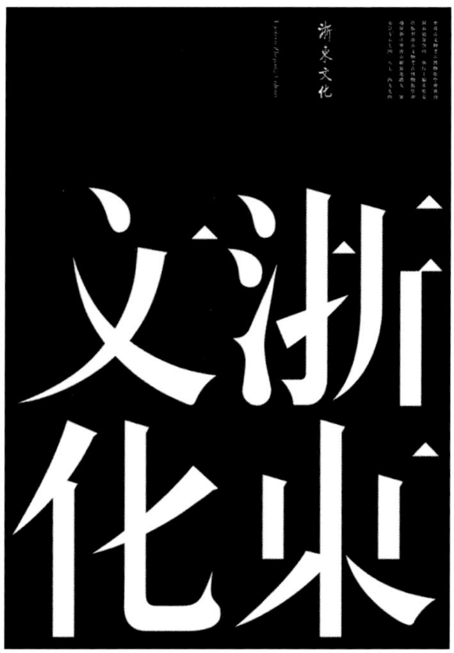

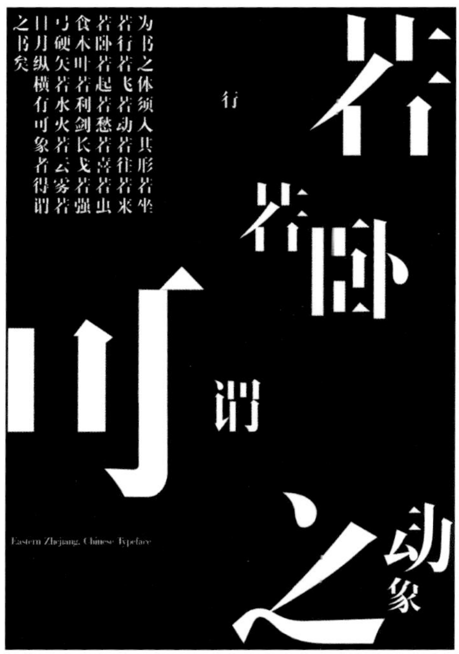

45 **Jiang Hua, Pan Qin**
The Exhibition of Art + Design / Suzhou Image
2002

46 **Jiang Hua**
Eastern Zhejiang Culture
浙東文化 2004

47 **Jiang Hua**
Scholar forum / Faculty of Communication and Arts,
Ningbo University, 2004

48 **Jiang Hua**
Eastern Zhejiang Chinese Typeface
2004

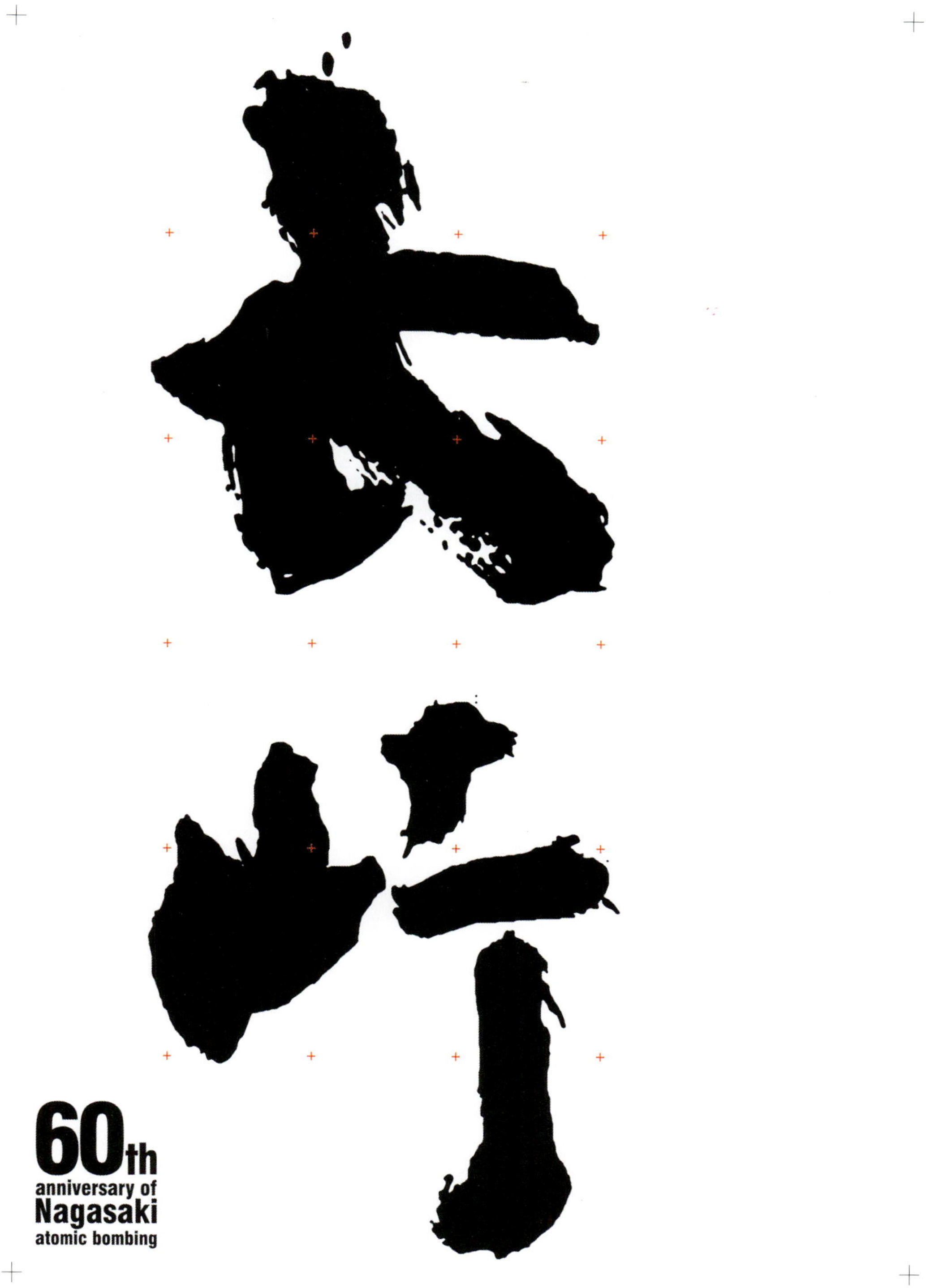

49 **Wang Xu**
60th Anniversary of Nagasaki Atomic Bombing
永嶒 "Nagasaki"
2005

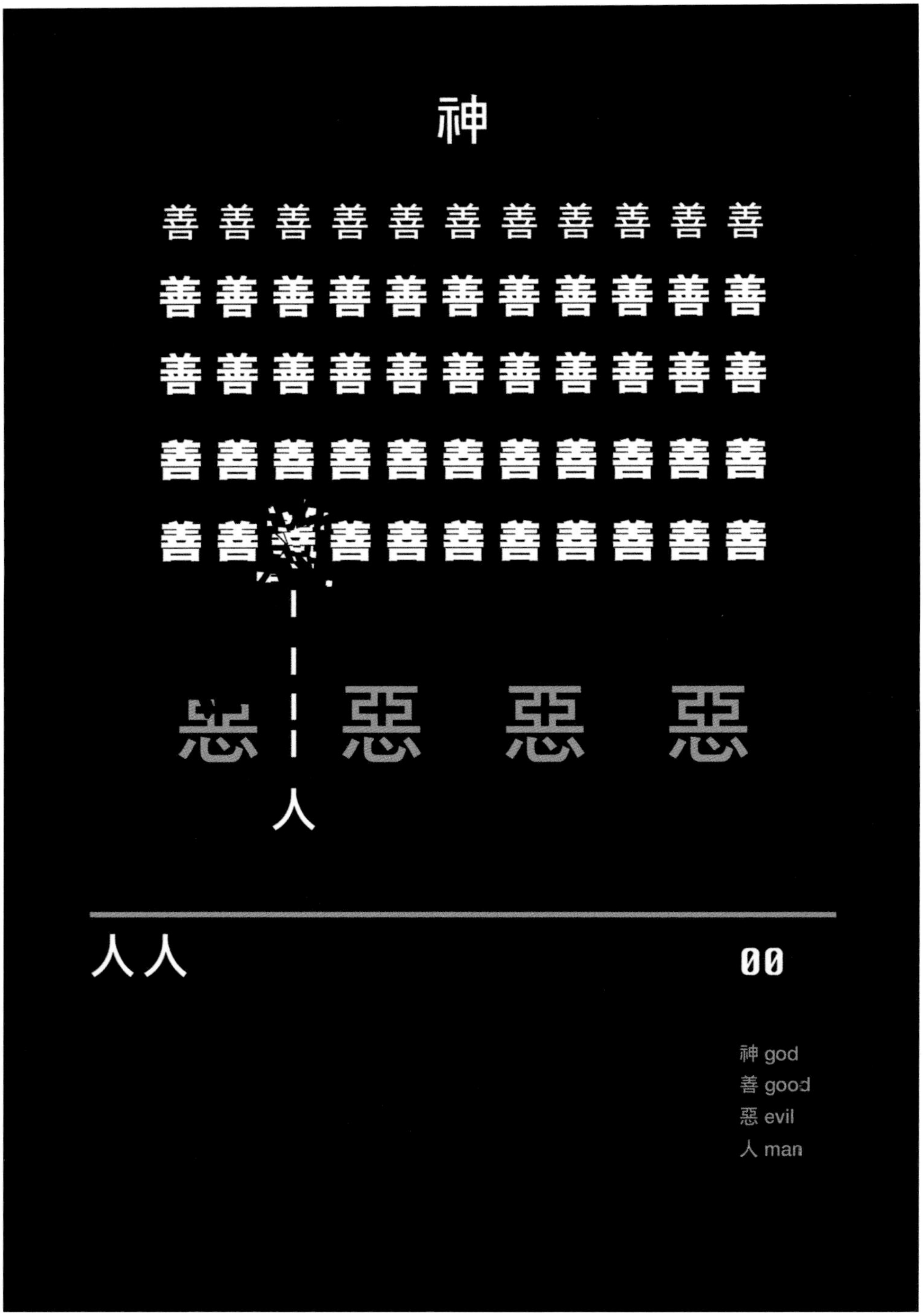

50 **Joseph Foo, Robin Koh**
Mensch & Gott – Man & God
1996

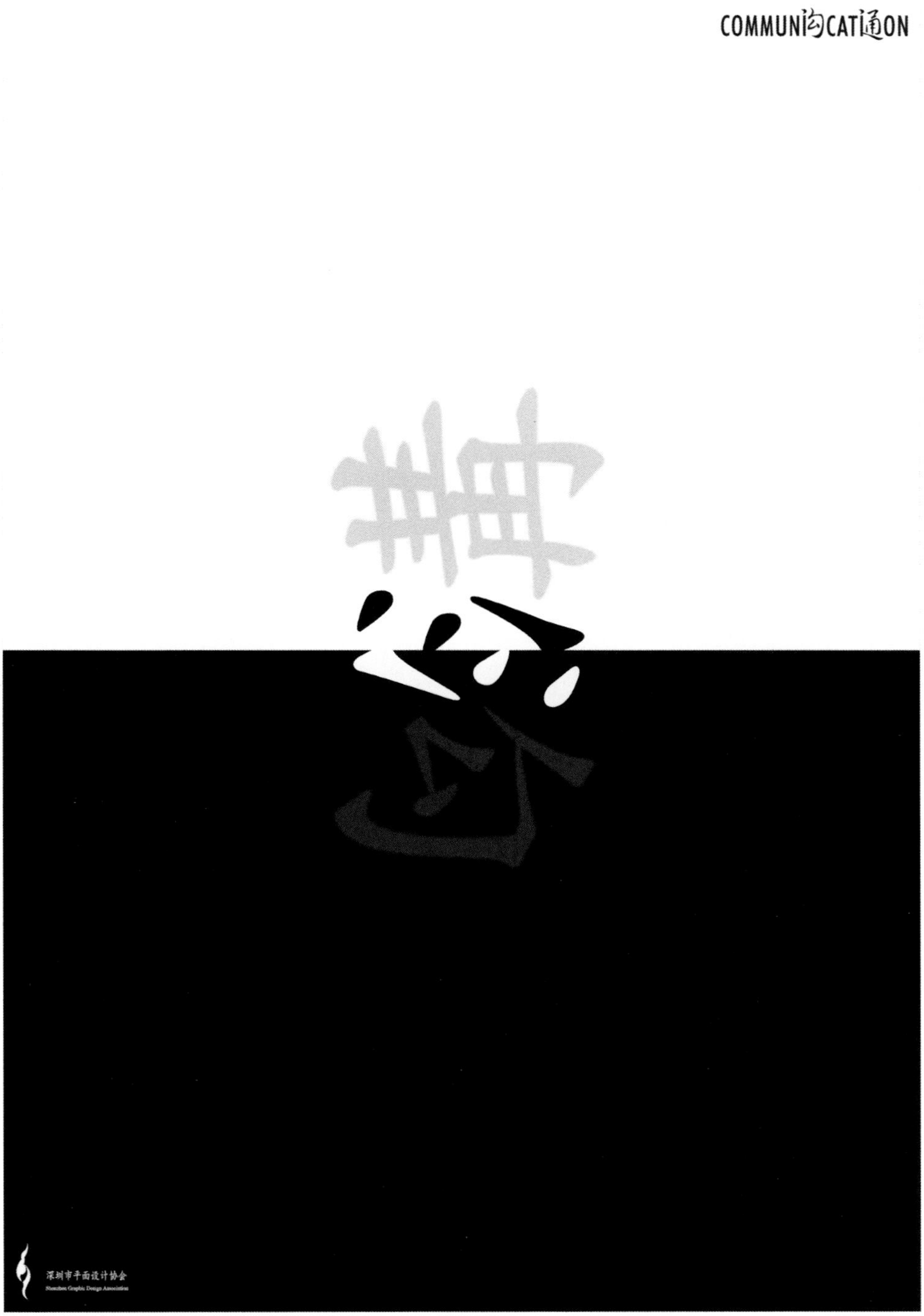

51 **Chen Shaohua**
Communication
沟通
1996

TYPO CHINA

Eva Lüdi Kong

Chinese characters are omnipresent in China's urban landscape. Whole rows of shop names over store windows or neon lettering for multi-storey restaurant façades adorn city buildings. Megaprint advertising posters conceal the last ruins of modest low buildings with tiled roofs that defined the cityscape until two decades ago. "Find the individual way" insists a clothing brand poster in powerful, forward-thrusting characters. "Let us work together to build up the fatherland" can be read in bald print on the walls round a building site in a new apartment block quarter. And high on the roof of a skyscraper that has only just shot up out of the ground, giant characters four metres high confidently promote themselves by proclaiming: "The future lies in my hand."

The new self-confidence attendant on the enormous country's economic success is the ground on which young Chinese graphic artists are increasingly realizing their own ideas. They are also finding it ever easier to tackle the wide range of interlinking standards and values, creating a field of tension in which people think and feel: traditional and new; individualism driven by Western values and ideas of cohesion firmly rooted in state and family; the fading socialist ideals that have been transformed into visions of a great future and the consumer promises of the market economy that now permeates everything, building up hopes of ideal worlds.

A glance at the recent past shows how young the new Chinese poster art actually is, apart from early examples of commercial posters in 1920s colonial Shanghai and the state propaganda posters that took their place in the three decades after the founding of the People's Republic in 1949. Chinese academies and colleges have been offering graphic design classes only since the mid 1980s. But there too it played a subordinate role for years as a sub-section within the «decorative arts» department, where the examination hurdles were set lower than for fine art subjects like oil painting, sculpture or traditional Chinese painting. In was in those reputable art subjects that the trainee artists of the day started to break away from the uniform, content-driven, realistic painting style the state insisted on, and began to unmask sanctimoniousness and take up personal attitudes. But in the course of the 1990s, as the opening and reform policy brought about the commercialization of urban centres, and the new consumer world was starting to impinge on people's lives, those values became less important. It suddenly seemed possible to buy happiness, and money threatened to become the key yardstick for value. The advertising industry was urgently seeking trained graphic artists, and graphic design became heavily subscribed, as a major subject that now offered lucrative prospects. After decades of artistic ideas driven by an ideologically determined ethic, a considered approach to poster design was just one challenge among others. Posters from Hongkong and

Taiwan offered an early benchmark. Here graphic design had been promoted as early as the 1960s, and shaped by influences from abroad. In these capitalistic centres of Chinese culture, which had remained untouched by the hostility to tradition promoted by the Cultural Revolution (1966–1976), the advertising industry had developed above all during the economic upsurge of the 1970s. Such forerunners, soon followed by examples from European countries, were at first extensively copied in the People's Republic–completely following the traditional Chinese didactic pattern which sets great store by imitating the masters. In this way the up-and-coming designers learned to move quickly and adroitly amid the chaos of new standards, to take up international trends while at the same time pursuing the needs of the Chinese market.

The international poster biennales and graphic design competitions that had proliferated since the 1990s opened the gates to international success. Young graphic artists fighting for recognition soon developed a refined sense of how to respond to juries' preferences. Occasionally, the emphasis on Chinese characters could be an indication that a design was being created for non-Chinese eyes. In this respect, that generation's opportunism ultimately worked in its own best interests–traditional values, unduly neglected for a time for political reasons, regained their actual value not least via the detour of a Western view. Now, as China becomes Westernized through "globalization", we can observe a return to its own cultural values at the same time: this applies in particular to the traditional arts and to the philosophies of Taoism and Confucianism.

Designers with a wide range of abilities are sought after in the People's Republic, offering everything from corporate design via advertising to title page design. The demand for posters is restricted to advertising, however, public commissions remain the exception. It is only in recent years that small numbers of non-commercial posters have been produced, for cultural events, for example. Under these circumstances, designing posters has developed partly as a kind of leisure pursuit. Graphic and fine artists often express themselves on themes they have chosen themselves and present their results for a restricted circle, at national graphics biennales, for example. This also explains why by far the greatest number of ambitious posters scarcely get any public exposure. But the trend towards typography that made itself felt in Hongkong and Taiwan about a decade earlier is manifesting itself ever more clearly in the Chinese media. Chinese characters appear more and more as an autonomous design device, especially on television.

The script, which traditional Chinese calligraphy placed under the highest artistic requirements, was for decades largely degraded to convey the ideological messages in the People's Republic. In the late 1980s, contemporary artists tried to re-accommodate the characters, for example by imitating the Cultural Revolution's large-format wall lettering in a purposely absurd manner, or by designing whole fonts of non-existent, unintelligible characters. In the posters collected here, typography using Chinese characters acquires its due weight from new approaches.

Unlike alphabetical script, whose letters exist solely as sounds and are assembled into words and sentences, the Chinese script system expresses a rich and highly interesting semantic culture. The individual character is highly expressive visually, and looks like an abstract image to outsiders, with elements that are encapsulated within, piled on top of or arranged next to each other, apparently without a beginning or an end. Each character represents a pictorial statement. Essentially, it is to be read as an object we look at and name at the same time; it virtually IS the object.

Anyone learning to read and write Chinese characters is setting off on a journey through the traces of times long past: they will learn to recognise images of the sun and moon, images of heaven and earth, of hand, foot, eye and mouth. Each new ideograph teaches the learner to recognize something more within the complex interplay of elements relating to meaning and phonetics, and of the all-embracing logic inherent in the Chinese script system, which seems to have evolved with such an easy grace. Essentially, this script divides the world up: everything fluid and wet is allocated «water» to convey its meaning, for example 河 *hé* ("river"), 海 *hǎi* ("sea"), 汁 *zhī* ("juice"), 浴 *yù* ("bath"). Everything that burns or cooks is characterized by "fire", for example 热 *rè* ("hot"), 焦 *jiāo* ("charred"), 煮 *zhǔ* ("cook")... And cows and dogs, horses and tigers, fish and birds constantly crop up as character components, remnants of a distant time that live on silently in China's everyday life, fitting in with the modern world astonishingly smoothly.

Certain characters are taken back to their original, concrete message in different works, with the pictorial quality often represented in an alienated way. In *One-m² field* (54), Liu Zhizhi fills the empty areas of the character田*tián* ("field") with light green areas of grass, thus creating an unusual negative view that at the same time restores the original pictorial message. Stanley Wong (41, 43) is taking a similar approach when he replaces the pictographic components of characters with photographic illustrations making the same statement. Here the reader's eye is alienated by the image's undue clarity, and the viewer's eye is disturbed by a distorted statement from the remaining character element.

The fact that script and image complement and run into each other is nothing new in China. It was always customary in both traditional ink painting and also in the popular illustrative art of the woodcut for the picture area to have lettering on it, so that the script was an inherent part of the image. He Jianping borrows directly from this tradition for his work *New Graphic* (7), placing the characters as representational elements in a landscape photograph in the style of ink painting.

Working with Chinese script inevitably also leads to traditional calligraphy, which is seen as one of the highest art forms in China. Here neither a decorative nor an ornamental approach is required, the key is in fact the expressive power within the lines' lively movement and a diverse and harmonious interplay of black and white. Jiang Hua defines calligraphy as the nodal point in Chinese art and the key to graphic design. Other graphic artists also appeal to this traditional medium in their designs and sometimes employ the black characters drawn with a paintbrush directly, as an expressive device.
Wang Xu has created two impressive works, *60th Anniversary of Atomic Bombing* (49), highly expressive posters each containing two large characters, black on white. Their message is sensually intelligible to viewers, regardless of whether or not they can read the script.

In the Chinese cultural sphere, script is important as a vehicle for culture. For Chinese viewers it is not just its pictorial richness that evokes direct associations with cultural contexts, but also its various styles and manifestations. Chen Shaohua's poster on the subject of communication (51) employs simple devices to create rich fields of association. The picture area is divided into black and white, evoking the universal polarity of Yin and Yang, recognizable visually as light and dark or heaven and earth. In the middle are two versions of the character *gōu* for "ditch", which forms part of the word "communication" in the sense of a free flow of information. At the top it appears as the traditional character 溝, and below in the simplified 沟 form used in the People's Republic since 1950. The component standing for «water» in the two signs remains the same, and forms the small visual field in which communication almost seems to take place, where white and black visibly shade into each other, while the adjacent parts of the character are already in the compound colour grey. Chen is also trying to establish communication between East and West, in addition to the symbolism of Yin-Yang and Classical-Modern by combining the English word "communication" with the corresponding Chinese characters 沟通 *gōu tōng*.

Despite the significance of the Chinese script tradition, by no means all designers exploit the ideograph's development history. Many of them prefer to come closer to printed script as captured in computer fonts. Here script is often handled in a way more akin to Western typography, like for example trying out minimal legibility by showing only half the characters, allowing the strokes to fall apart or consistently omitting all the horizontal strokes (46–48). One instance is Bob Chen's (6) poster *Four* for a paper manufacturer, on which the character for the word "four" appears as a large, white expanse like a blank sheet of paper. The ideograph can still be read without difficulty via the outlines that the character's complex structure creates.

The Roman alphabet, widespread in China thanks to official *Pinyin* transliteration and the inevitability of the English language, also appears in graphic works from time to time. Against the background of Chinese characters, letters in general are perceived as signs without souls, abstract structures relating only to sound, unable to define any Chinese character adequately because of the transliteration's lack of pictorial content.

Overall, the posters in this selection present us with a wealth of graphic treatment forms for script. It sometimes seems that as the range of what is expected expands all too rapidly, everything has become possible, everything is present at the same time. At present China's visual culture is in a particular phase of development, with hopeful prospects opening up. And yet experts complain of inadequacies in Chinese graphic design, especially as far as standards for day-to-day use are concerned. Wang Xu defines the omnipresent creations intended to suit mass taste as "fast food style". He regrets that the proportion of ambitious design is too low, and that good work is scarcely acknowledged. Criticism is also made of the mindless copying of Western models, which continues to be widespread, and this often goes hand in hand with traditional elements exploited superficially. He also points out the shortage of qualified teachers for training purposes.

For many designers, coming to terms with tradition remains a bright spot. Thinking back like this is part of the hope that it will at last be possible to present independent ideas in an international context, after a period of one-sided Western influence. It is also desirable that a real culture of commissioning ambitious design can be established in the People's Republic.

The graphic posters presented under the title *Typo China* remain mysterious and encoded in many respects in Western eyes. And yet it is precisely the Chinese characters, their pictorial quality and expressiveness, that make both reading and merely looking at the posters a fascinating experience–feeling our way into a cultural atmosphere that is still too unfamiliar, and that can enrich our experience well beyond the graphic and visual field.

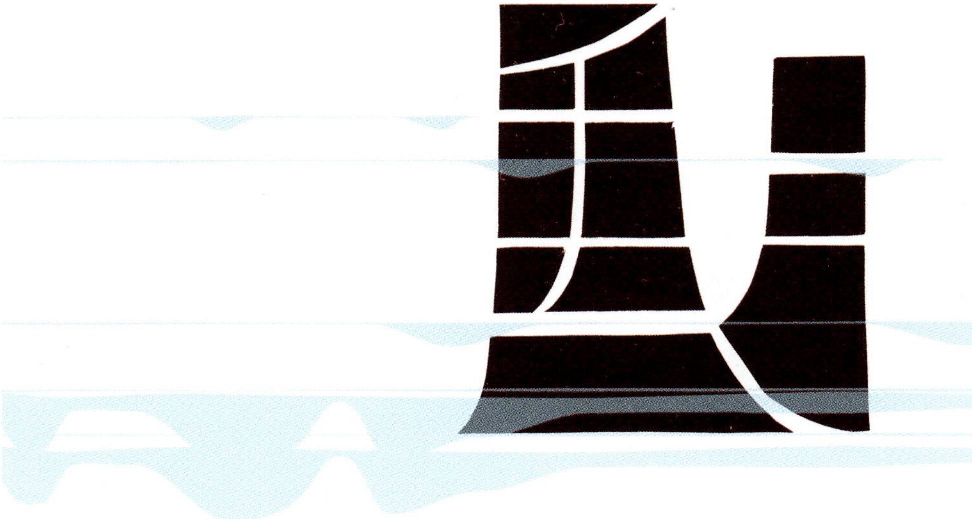

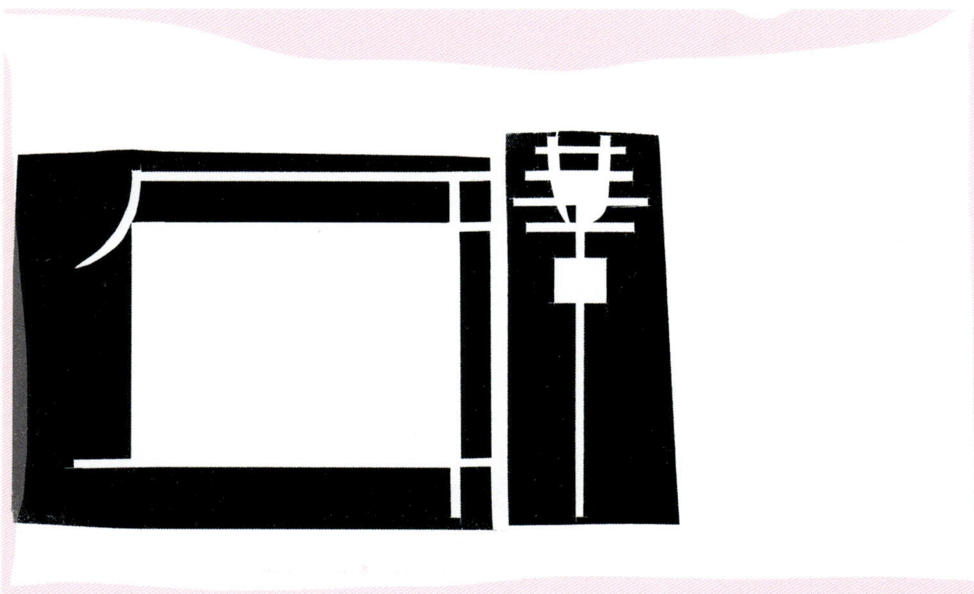

52/53 **Guang Yu**
"The wind and moon are timeless, but youth and beauty are restricted by boundries"
52: 風 "Wind", 月 «Mond» – "moon"
53: 年 «Jahr» – "year", 華 «Jugend» – "youth"
2004

54 **Liu Zhizhi**
Living Tea Table / One-m² field / Mima Café Beijing
田 «Feld» – “field”
2004

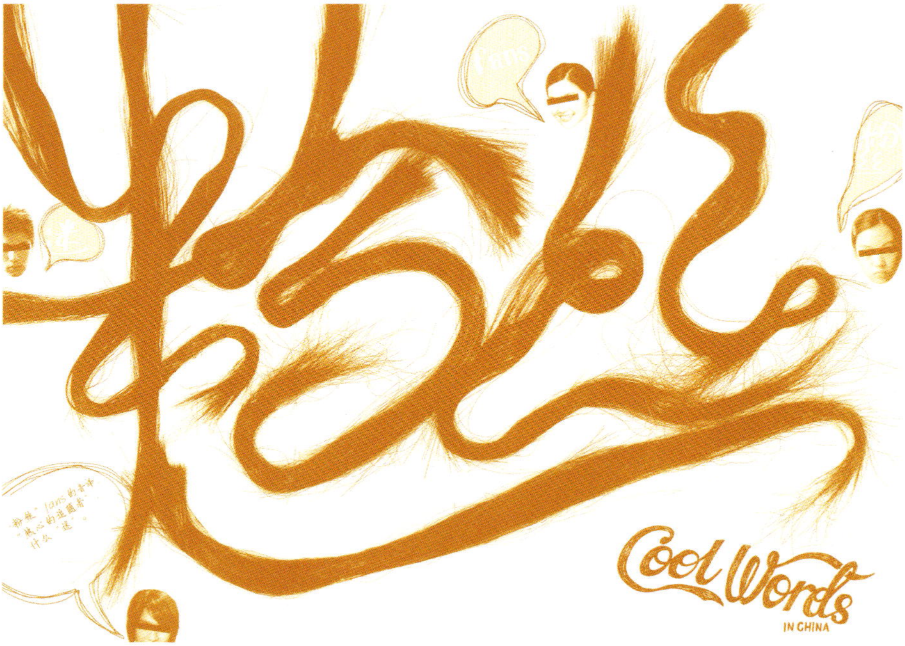

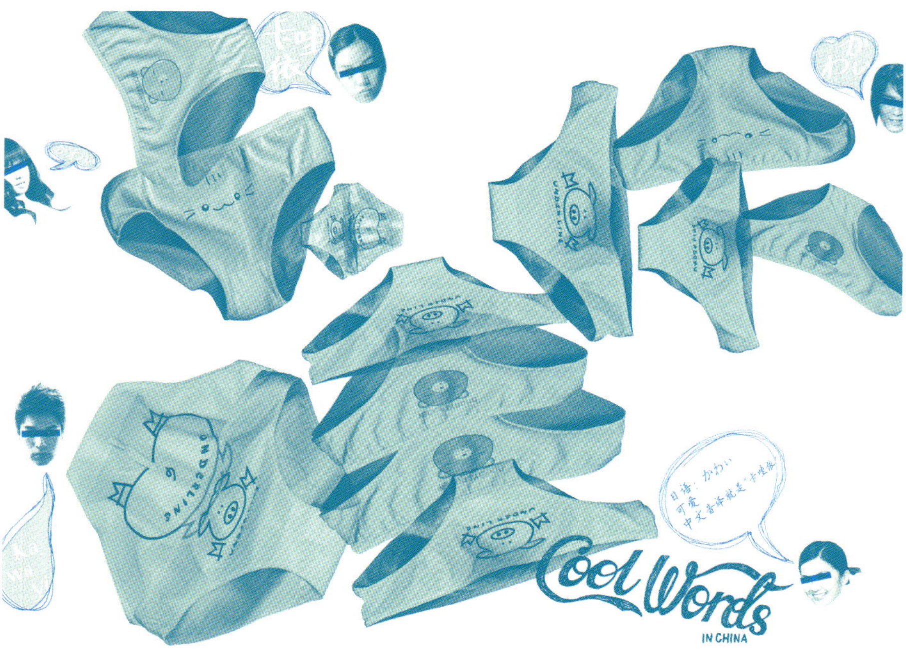

55 **Xia Wenxi**
Cool words in China/Fans
粉丝
2005

56 **Xia Wenxi**
Cool words in China/kawayi
卡哇衣
2005

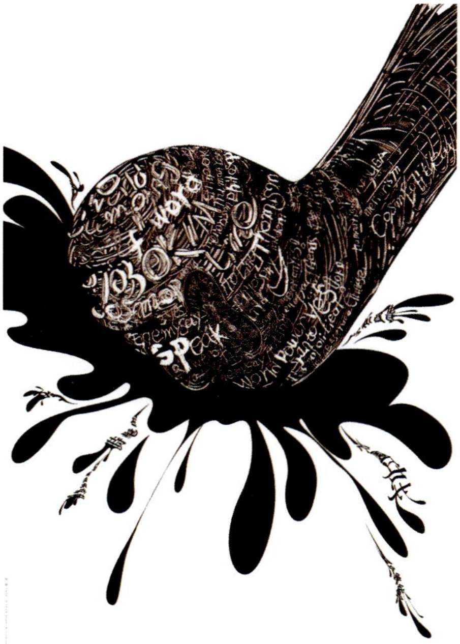

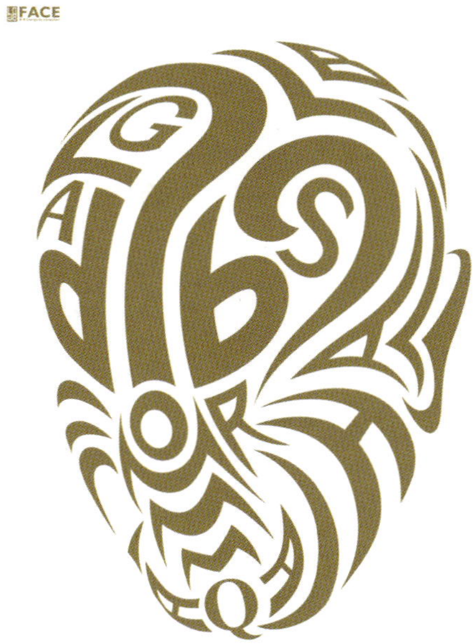

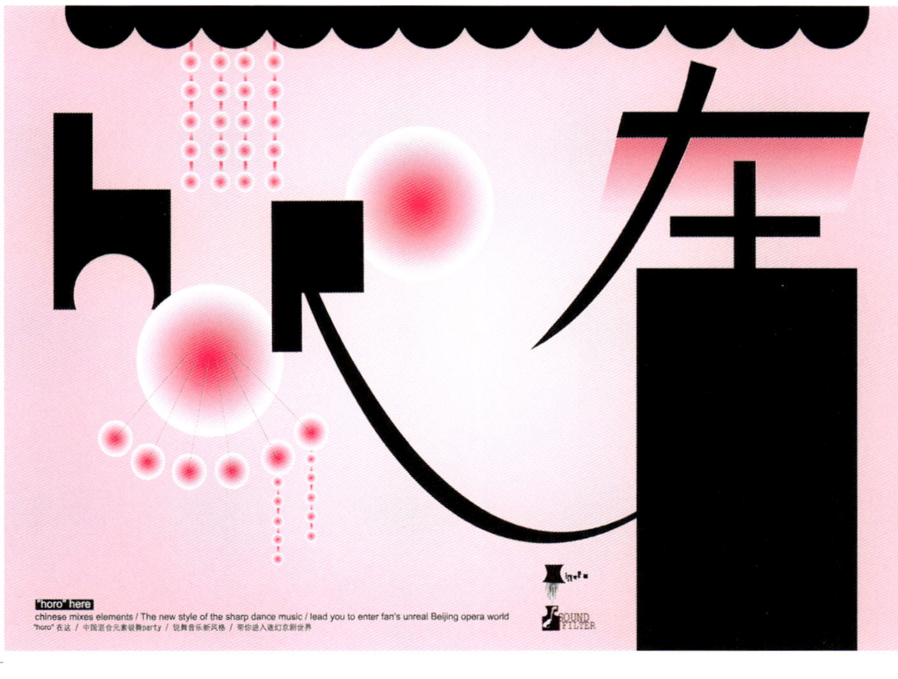

57 **Yang Zhen**
Face to face, 2003

58 **Bai Zhiwei**
Horo here/the new style of the sharp dance music
在这
2004

59 **Yang Zhen**
Face
2003

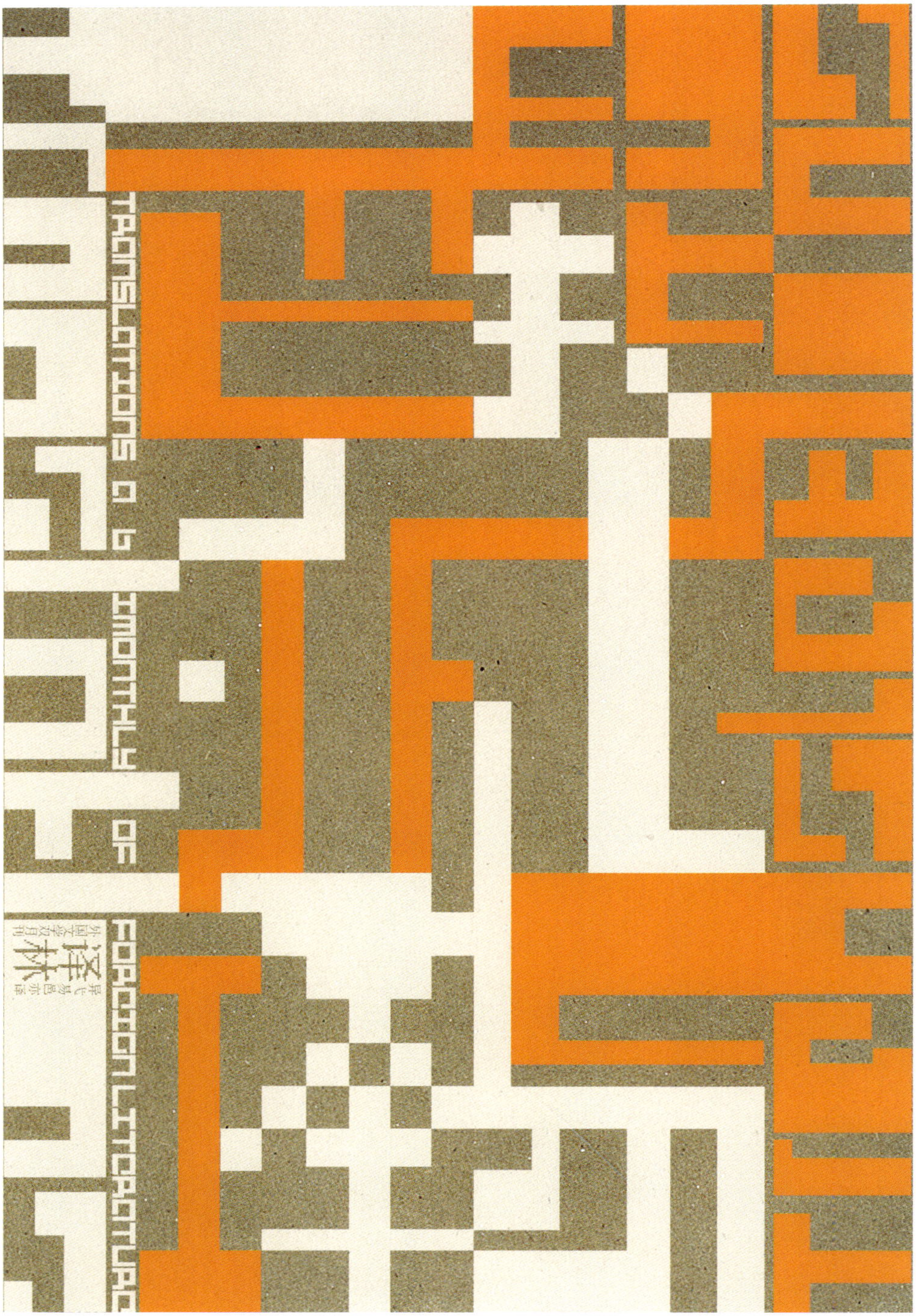

60 **Zhao Qing**
Translations/A bimonthly of foreign literature
2005

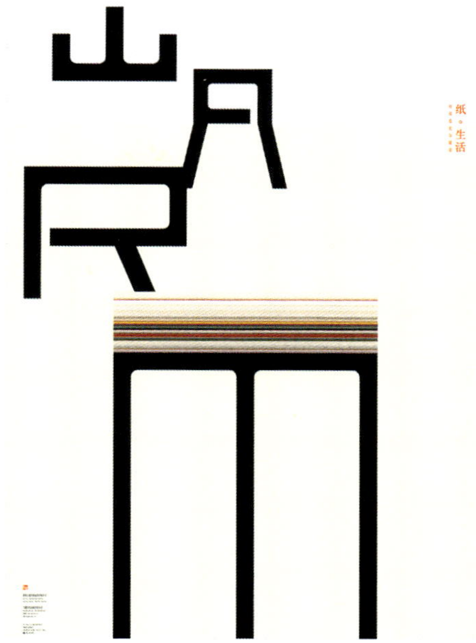

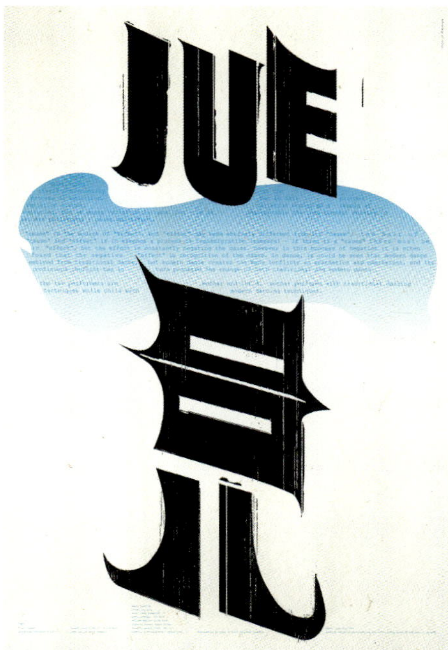

61 **Au Tak-shing**
War/Warm, 2003

62 **Liu Zhizhi**
Jue/Dance and music
Haus der Kulturen der Welt, Berlin
覺 2004

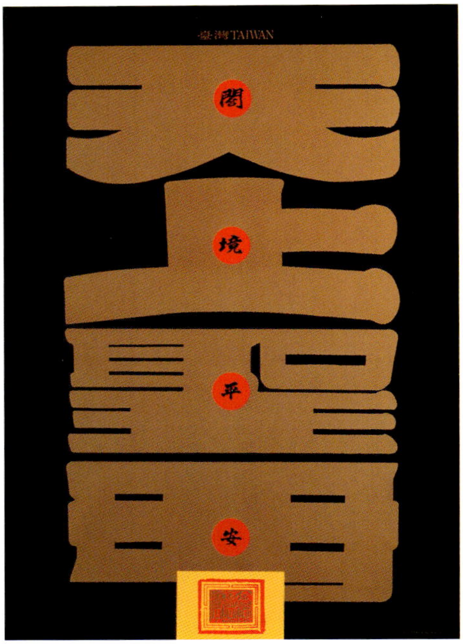

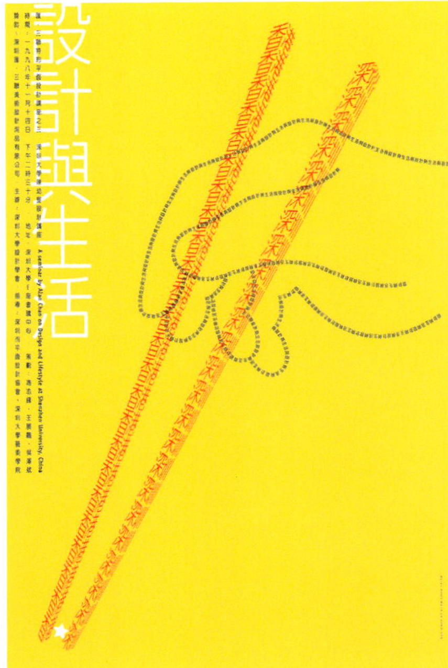

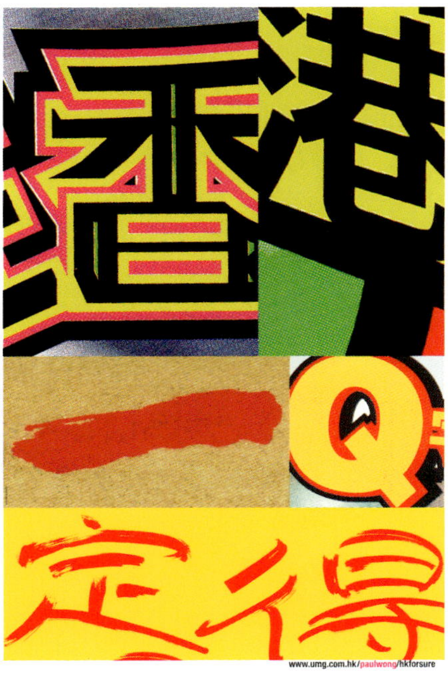

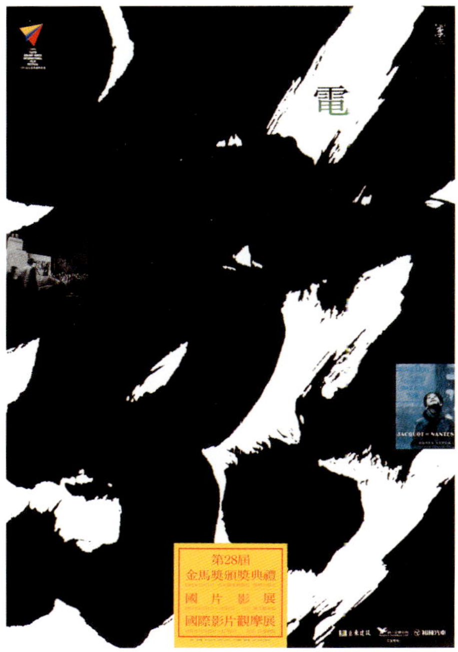

63 **Yu Ming-Lung**
Göttin – Goddess
[Ausstellungsplakat – Exhibition poster]
天上聖母 1995

64 **Sandy Choi**
Paul Wong, 2000

65 **Alan Chan**
Design & Leben – Design & Life
設計與生活 «Design und Leben» – “Design and Life”
香港 “Hongkong” 深圳 “Shenzhen”, 1998

66 **Yu Ming-Lung**
Taipei 28th Golden Horse International Film Festival, 1991

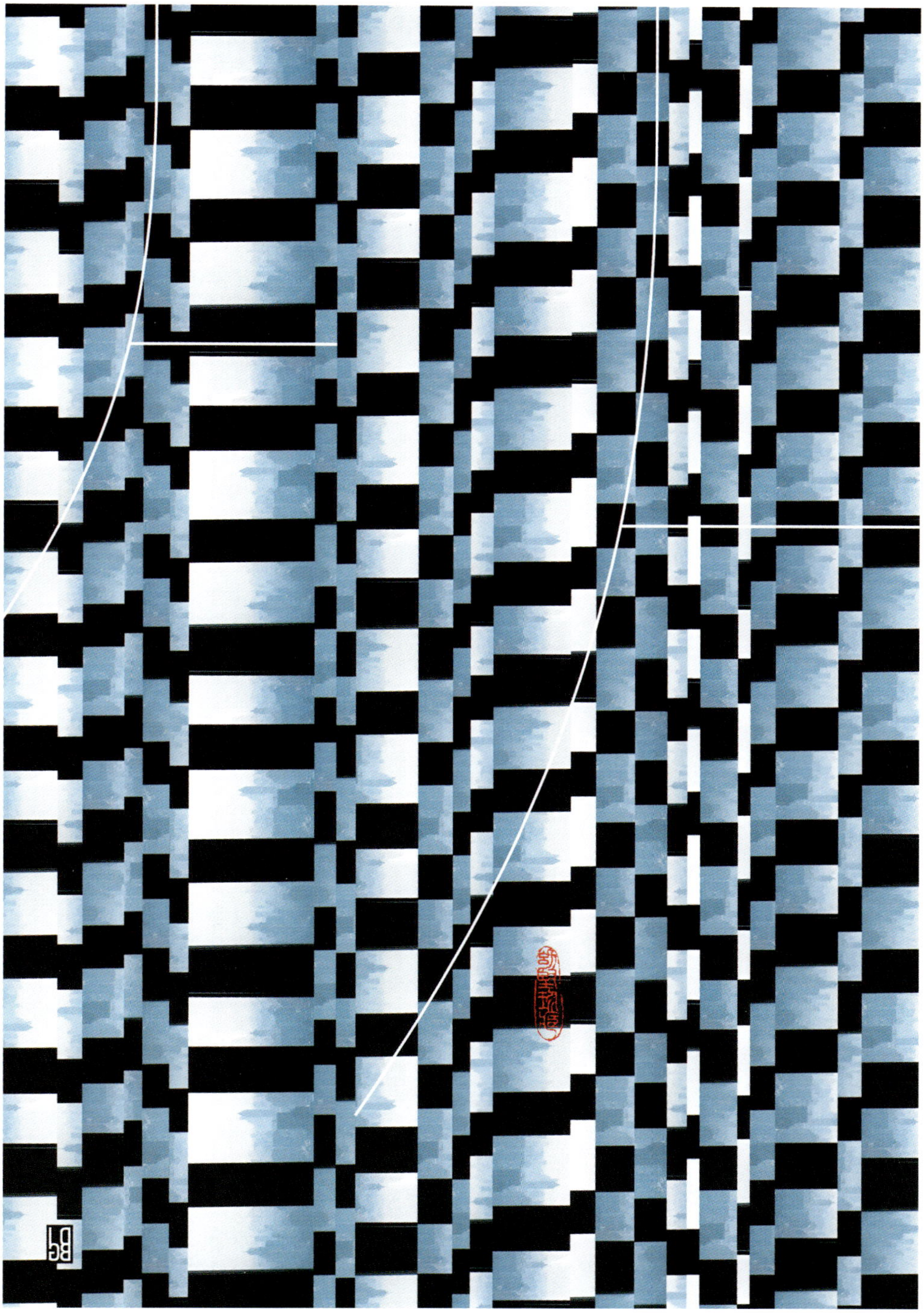

67 **Alan Chan**
In love with bamboo
竹
2005

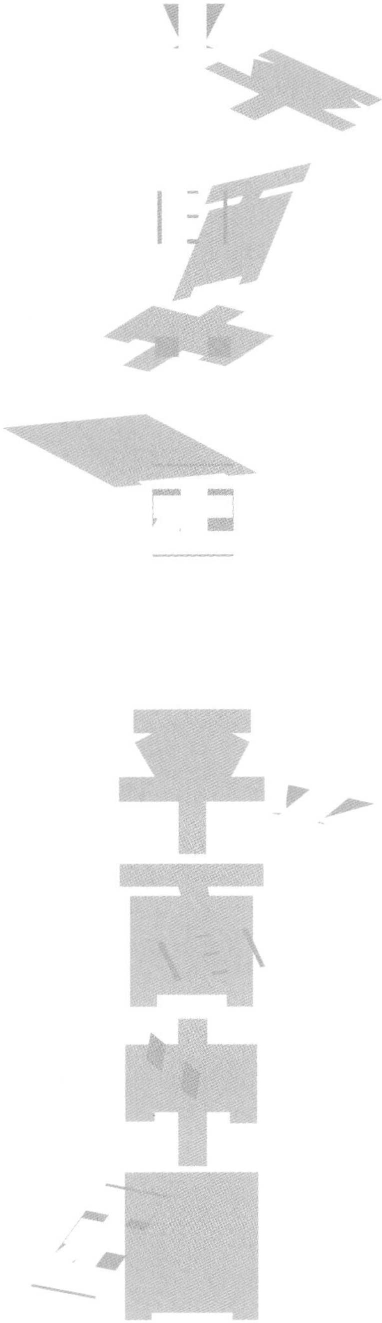

68/69 **Bob Chen**
China Graphic
平面中国
2004

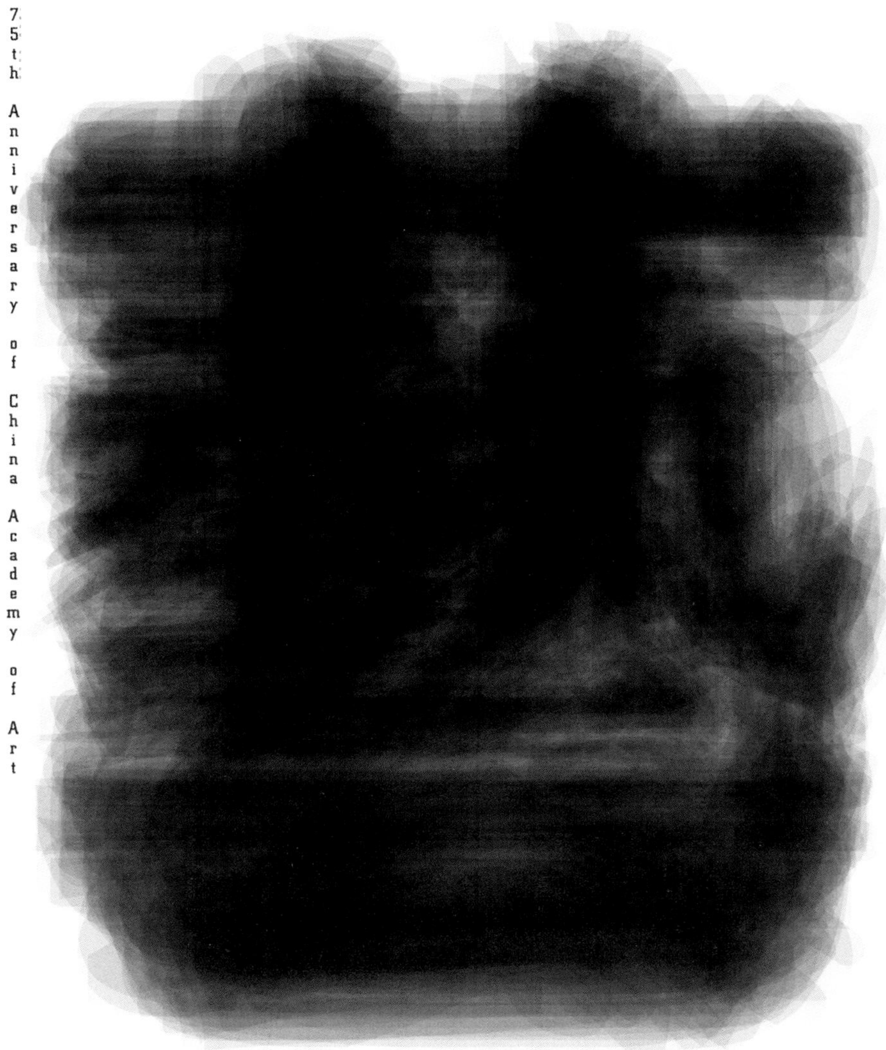

70 **He Jianping**
75th Anniversary of China Academy of Art
藝術 «Kunst» – “Art”
2003

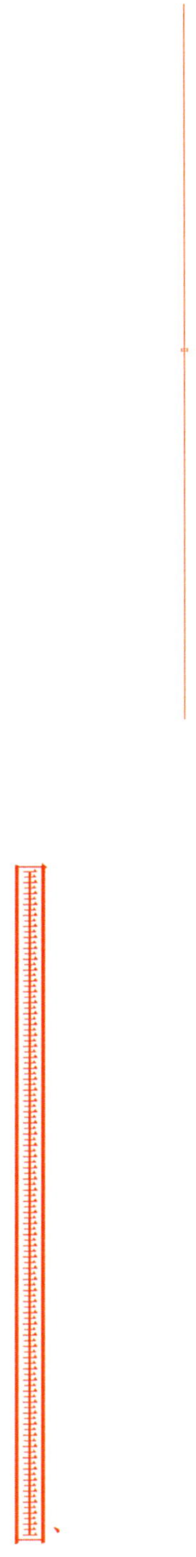

71/72 **Chen Guojin**
In China
中 国 “China”
2004

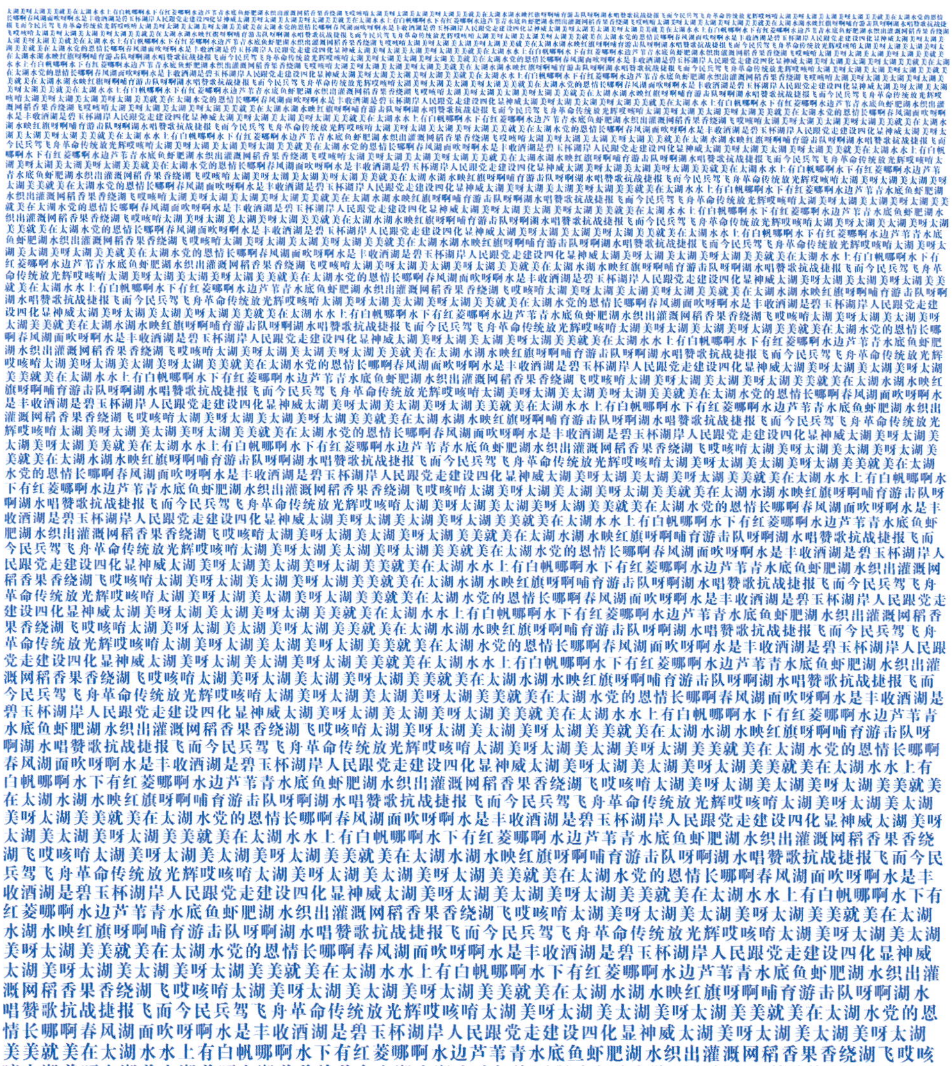

73 **Jiang Hua, Pan Qin**
Tai Lake/Suzhou Image
2003

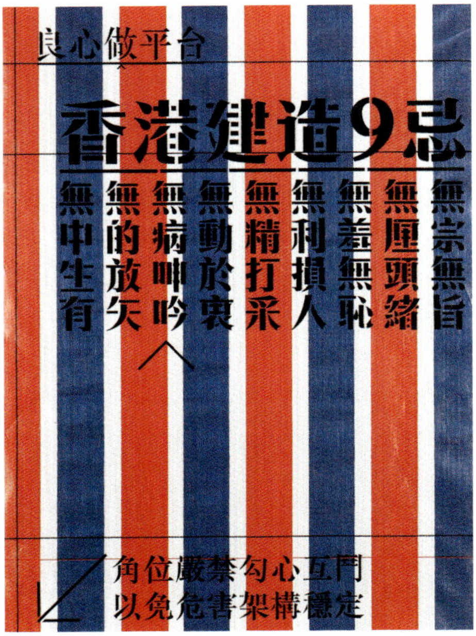

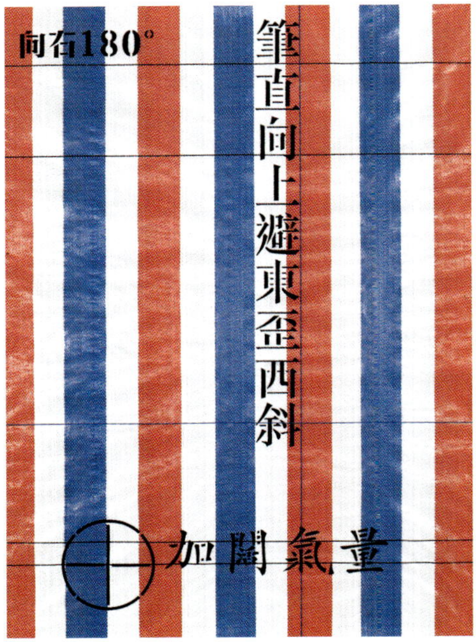

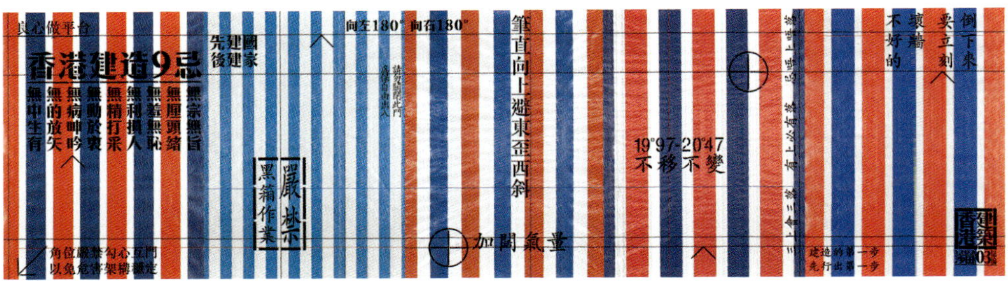

74–77 **Stanley Wong**
Building Hongkong
2003

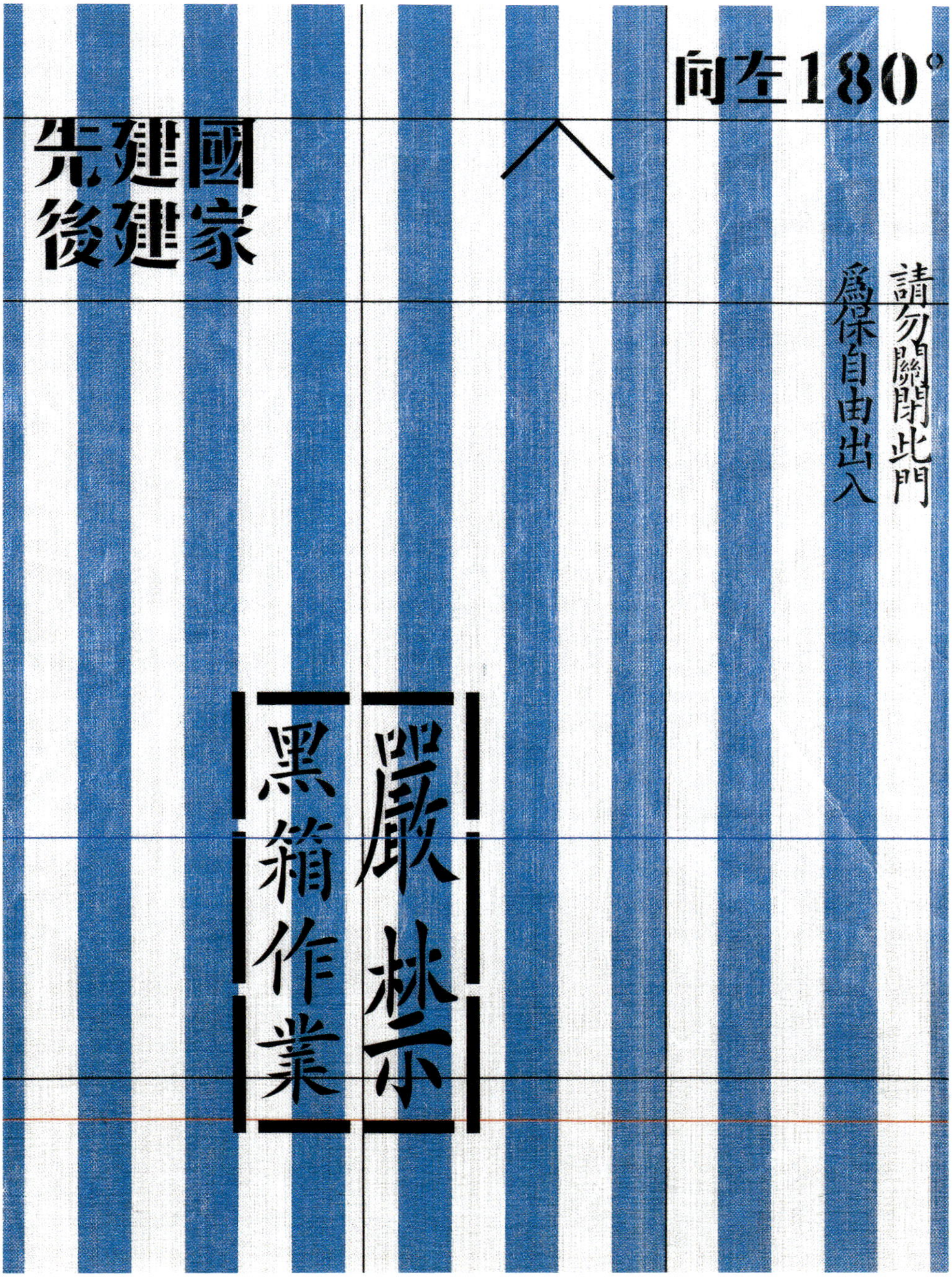
向左180°
先建國
後建家
請勿關閉此門
爲保自由出入
嚴禁
黑箱作業

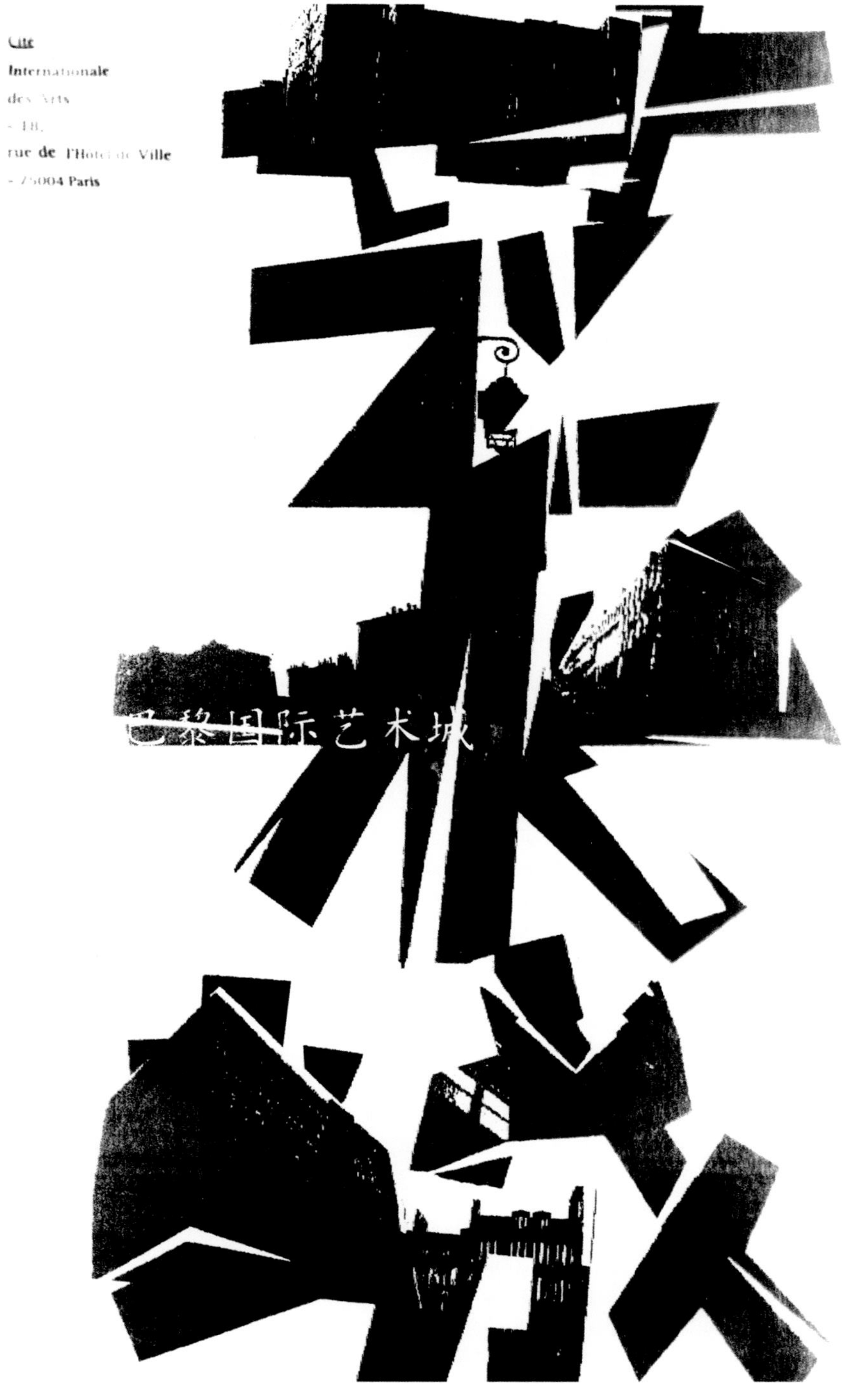

78 **Bi Xuefeng**
Paris, Cité Internationale des Arts
艺术城 «Stadt der Künste» – “City of Arts”
2005

Katalog

Alle abgebildeten Plakate stammen aus der Plakatsammlung des Museums für Gestaltung Zürich, mit Ausnahme von Nr. 74 bis 77.

Die Daten des Katalogs folgen den Rubriken Gestaltung, Plakattext, Erscheinungsjahr, Erscheinungsland, Drucktechnik und Format. Dabei gelten folgende Regelungen:

Gestaltung: Es wird der vollständige Name in chinesischer Schreibweise (Nachname, Vorname) angegeben.

Plakattext: Die beste Textwiedergabe bildet die Abbildung des Plakates selbst. Darum wird hier eine vereinfachte Form wiedergegeben, welche nur die aussagekräftigen Textbestandteile berücksichtigt. Allfällige Umstellungen dienen der Verständlichkeit. Das Zeichen/trennt inhaltliche Texteinheiten. Die chinesischen Schriftzeichen werden dort wiedergegeben, wo sie zur zentralen Aussage des Plakats gehören.

Erscheinungsland: Das Erscheinungsland wird mit dem international gebräuchlichen ISO-Code angegeben: CN für die Volksrepublik China, MY für Malaysia und TW für Taiwan.

Format: Die Angaben werden in der Abfolge Höhe × Breite und in cm gemacht. Weil Plakate oft nicht exakt rechtwinklig geschnitten sind, werden die Abmessungen auf halbe cm aufgerundet.

Die Plakatgeschichte ist ein junges Forschungsgebiet – verlässliche Hinweise sind rar. Jeder Hinweis und jede Ergänzung sind willkommen:
Plakatsammlung@museum-gestatung.ch

Catalogue

All the posters illustrated with the exception of nos. 74 to 77 are from the Museum für Gestaltung Zürich's Poster Collection.

The data in the catalogue are under the headings poster text, year of appearance, country of first appearance, printing technique, format. The following rules have been applied:

Design: The full name is given following Chinese practice (surname, first name).

Poster text: the poster itself provides the best version of the text. Thus a simplified form is used here, giving only the most meaningful elements of the text. Any rearrangements that have been made are for purposes of intelligibility. The sign/separates textual units by content.
Chinese characters are reproduced where they form part of the poster's central statement.

Country of first appearance: the country in which the poster appeared is identified by the internationally accepted ISO Code:
CN for the People's Republic of China, MY for Malaysia and TW for The Republic of China/Taiwan.

Format: the details are given in the sequence height × width and in cm. Because posters are often not cut exactly at right angles, the dimensions are rounded off to half cm.

The history of posters is a recent field of research – reliable information is rare. Any references or additional material are welcome:
plakat.sammlung@museum-gestaltung.ch

1 He Jianping
China
中國
2005
CN Siebdruck – screenprint
120 × 89,5 cm

2 He Jun
Beauty of Books/6th Chinese Exhibition of Book Design
2005
CN Offset 100 × 70 cm

3 Han Jiaying
Frontiers
美
«schön» – "beautiful"
1997 1/3
CN Offset 100 × 70 cm

4 Chen Guojin
Neun Leben – Nine Lives
九生
2004
CN Offset 80 × 57 cm

5 Li Yingwei
Design Shenzhen / Schnelle Entwicklung – Rapid Development
2003
CN Offset 100 × 70 cm

6 Bob Chen
Vier – Four
肆
2005
CN Siebdruck – screenprint
120 × 90 cm

7 He Jianping
New Graphic [Design Magazine]
新平面
2003
CN Offset 100 × 70 cm

8 Zhang Wanbao
3D Font, 2003
CN Offset 100 × 70 cm

9 Ye Changchun
AD 518 New Year's Carnival / Qinghua University
2004
CN Offset 90 × 60 cm

10 Lam Hung
Chinese Character
Erfundene Zeichen für – Invented characters for: internet, e-mail, mouse, printer, computer, pdf
2003
CN Offset 100 × 70 cm

11 Lam Hung
Peace of Mind – Zenter
心 «Herz» – "Heart"
2001
CN Offset 102,5 × 72 cm

12 Tsang Kin-wah
Untitled
2004 1/3
CN Siebdruck – screenprint
96 × 64 cm

13 Bai Zhiwei
Welterbe Suzhou / Brücke – Heritage of the world Suzhou / Bridge
2004 1/2
CN Offset 100 × 70 cm

14 Zhao Qing
Typography
2005 1/2
CN Offset 100 × 70 cm

15 Bai Zhiwei
Welterbe Suzhou / Fluss – Heritage of the World Suzhou / Stream
2004 2/2
CN Offset 100 × 70 cm

16 Zhao Qing
Typography
2005 2/2
CN Offset 100 × 70 cm

17 Chen Yuanchuan
Pinsel / Pinselhalter – Brush / rack
筆
2000
CN Offset 91 × 68 cm

18 Han Jiaying
Fusion
1999 1/2
CN Offset 100 × 70 cm

19 Chen Yuanchuan
Chinese Artistic Conception
2000
CN Offset 100 × 70 cm

20 Han Jiaying
Fusion
1999 2/2
CN Offset 100 × 70 cm

21 Bi Xuefeng
Typography
2004 1/2
CN Offset 100 × 70 cm

22 Bi Xuefeng
Typography
2004
CN Offset 65,5 × 94 cm

23 Bi Xuefeng
Typography
2004 2/2
CN Offset 100 × 70 cm

24 Han Jiaying
Frontiers
1999 1/4
CN Offset 100 × 70 cm

25 Han Jiaying
Frontiers
1999 2/4
CN Offset 100 × 70 cm

26 Han Jiaying
Frontiers
1999 3/4
CN Offset 100 × 70 cm

27 Han Jiaying
Frontiers
1999 4/4
CN Offset 100 × 70 cm

28 Han Jiaying
In China
2005 1/5
CN Offset 100 × 70 cm

29 Han Jiaying
In China
2005 2/5
CN Offset 100 × 70 cm

30 Han Jiaying
In China
2005 3/5
CN Offset 100 × 70 cm

31 Han Jiaying
In China
2005 4/5
CN Offset 100 × 70 cm

32 Han Jiaying
In China
2005 5/5
CN Offset 100 x 70 cm

33 Li Yingwei
In China
2005
CN Offset 100 × 70 cm

34 Pan Qin
The Exhibition of Exceptional Student Work / Ningbo University
2003
CN Siebdruck – screenprint
110 × 80 cm

35 Zhao Qing
Nanjing Image Cities
2005 1/2
CN Offset 100 × 70 cm

36 Zhao Qing
Hanqingtang Design
2005 1/4
CN Offset 100 × 70 cm

37 Zhao Qing
Hanqingtang Design
2005 2/4
CN Offset 100 × 70 cm

38 Zhao Qing
Hanqingtang Design
2005 3/4
CN Offset 100 × 70 cm

39 Zhao Qing
Hanqingtang Design
2005 4/4
CN Offset 100 × 70 cm

40 Wang Yuefei
"Take the branch for the Root"
本 «Ursprung» – "origin"
末 «Ende» – "end"
木 «Holz» – "wood"
2005 1/2
CN Siebdruck – screenprint
100 × 70 cm

41 Stanley Wong
Fuss – Foot
路 «Weg» – "path"
2003 9/9
CN Offset 100 × 70 cm

42 Wong Imaya
Mutter und Kind – Mother and child
母 «Mutter» – "Mother"
2005 1/2
MY Offset 100 × 70 cm

43 Stanley Wong
Auge – Eye
見 «sehen» – "to see"
2003 6/9
CN Offset 100 × 70 cm

44 Wong Imaya
Mutter und Kind – Mother and child
子 «Kind» – "child"
2005 2/2
MY Offset 100 × 70 cm

45 Jiang Hua, Pan Qin
The Exhibition of Art + Design/
Suzhou Image
2002
CN Offset 103 × 73 cm

46 Jiang Hua
Eastern Zhejiang Culture
[Literature Magazine]
浙東文化
2004
CN Offset 100 × 70 cm

47 Jiang Hua
Scholar forum/Faculty of
Communication and Arts, Ningbo
University
2004
CN Offset 103 × 73 cm

48 Jiang Hua
Eastern Zhejiang Chinese Typeface
2004
CN Offset 100 × 70 cm

49 Wang Xu
60th Anniversary of Nagasaki
Atomic Bombing
永皬 "Nagasaki"
2005 1/2
CN digital print 155 × 92 cm

50 Joseph Foo, Robin Koh
Mensch & Gott – Man & God
神 «Gott» – "God"
善 «Das Gute» – "Good"
惡 «Das Böse» – "Evil"
人 «Der Mensch» – "Man"
1996
MY Offset 100 × 70 cm

51 Chen Shaohua
Communication
沟通
1996
CN Offset 85 × 60 cm

52 Guang Yu
"The wind and moon are
timeless, but youth and beauty
are restricted by boundries"
風 "Wind", 月 «Mond» – "moon"
2004 1/2
CN Siebdruck/Reispapier
– screenprint/rice paper
63 × 100 cm

53 Guang Yu
"The wind and moon are
timeless, but youth and beauty
are restricted by boundries"
年 «Jahr» – "year",
華 «Jugend» – "youth"
2004 2/2
CN Siebdruck/Reispapier
– screenprint/rice paper
63 × 100 cm

54 Liu Zhizhi
Living Tea Table/One-m^2 field/
Mima Café Beijing
田 «Feld» – "field"
2004
CN Offset 100 × 70 cm

55 Xia Wenxi
Cool words in China/Fans
粉丝
2005
CN Offset 70 × 100 cm

56 Xia Wenxi
Cool words in China/kawayi
«Auf japanisch heisst kawayi
niedlich»
"In japanese kawayi means cute"
卡哇衣
2005
CN Offset 70 × 100 cm

57 Yang Zhen
Face to face
2003
CN Offset 100 × 70 cm

58 Bai Zhiwei
Horo here/the new style of the
sharp dance music
在这
2004 1/2
CN Offset 70 × 100 cm

59 Yang Zhen
Face
2003
CN Offset 100 × 70 cm

60 Zhao Qing
Translations/A bimonthly of
foreign literature
2005
CN Offset 100 × 70 cm

61 Au Tak-shing
War/Warm
2003
CN Offset 100 × 70 cm

62 Liu Zhizhi
Jue/Dance and music
Haus der Kulturen der Welt, Berlin
– House of World Cultures, Berlin
覺
2004
CN Offset 100 × 70 cm

63 Yu Ming-Lung
Göttin / Goddess
[Ausstellungsplakat – Exhibition
poster]
天上聖母
1995
TW Offset 98 × 70 cm

64 Sandy Choi
Paul Wong
2000
CN Offset 100 × 70 cm

65 Alan Chan
Design & Leben – Design & Life
設計與生活 «Design und Leben»
– "Design and Life"
香港 "Hongkong"
深圳 "Shenzhen"
1998
CN Offset 91 × 61 cm

66 Yu Ming-Lung
Taipei 28th Golden Horse
International Film Festival
1991
TW Offset 100 × 70 cm

67 Alan Chan
In love with bamboo
竹
2005 1/4
CN Offset 100 × 70 cm

68 Bob Chen
China Graphic
平面中国
2004 1/2
CN Offset 70 × 50 cm

69 Bob Chen
China Graphic
平面中国
2004 2/2
CN Offset 70 × 50 cm

70 He Jianping
75th Anniversary of China
Academy of Art
藝術 «Kunst» – "Art"
2003 1/2
CN Siebdruck – screenprint
119 x 84 cm

71/72 Chen Guojin
In China
中 国 "China"
2004 1/2 / 2/2
CN Offset 80 × 57 cm

73 Jiang Hua, Pan Qin
Tai Lake/Suzhou Image
2003
CN Siebdruck – screenprint
119 x 84 cm

74 Stanley Wong
Building Hongkong
2003 1/5
CN Siebdruck/Plastikgewebe – screenprint/plastic fabric
119 × 89 cm

75 Stanley Wong
Building Hongkong
2003 1–5
CN Siebdruck/Plastikgewebe – screenprint/plastic fabric
je/each 119 × 89 cm

76 Stanley Wong
Building Hongkong
2003 2/5
CN Siebdruck/Plastikgewebe – screenprint/plastic fabric
je/each 119 × 89 cm

77 Stanley Wong
Building Hongkong
2003 3/5
CN Siebdruck/Plastikgewebe – screenprint/plastic fabric
je/each 119 × 89 cm

78 Bi Xuefeng
Paris, Cité Internationale des Arts
艺术城 «Stadt der Künste» – "City of Arts"
2005
CN Offset 100 × 70 cm

Designer/Designers

AU Tak-shing, *1964 in Hongkong, lives in Hongkong.

BAI Zhiwei, *1981 in Shenzhen, lives in Shenzhen.

BI Xuefeng, *1963 in Heibei, lives in Shenzhen.

Alan CHAN, *1950 in Hongkong, lives in Hongkong.

Bob CHEN, *1979 in Putuo, Prov. Zhejiang, lives in Hangzhou.

CHEN Guojin, *1977 in Zhangjiang, lives in Shenzhen.

CHEN Shaohua, *1954 in Shangyu, Prov. Zhejiang, lives in Shenzhen.

CHEN Yuanchuan, *1969 in Wuxi, lives in Wuxi.

LAM Hung, *1973 in Hongkong, lives in Hongkong.

GUANG Yu, *1977 in Beijing, lives in Beijing.

HAN Jiaying, *1961 in Tianjin, lives in Shenzhen.

HE Jianping, *1973 in Fuyang, Prov. Zhejiang lives in Berlin and Shanghai.

HE Jun, *1977 in Qingdao, Prov. Shandong, lives in Beijing.

JIANG Hua, *1973 in Zhoushan, lives in Ningbo.

Joseph FOO, *1967 in Petaling Jaya, Malaysia, lives in Petaling Jaya, Malaysia.

LI Yingwei, *1977 in Prov. Shanxi, lives in Taiyuan.

LIU Zhizhi, *1975 in Beijing, lives in Beijing.

PAN Qin, *1967 in Zhejiang, lives in Ningbo.

Sandy CHOI, *1959 in Hongkong, lives in Hongkong.

Stanley WONG, *1960 in Hongkong, lives in Hongkong.

TSANG Kin-wah, *1976 in Hongkong, lives in Hongkong.

WANG Xu, *1955 in Guangzhou, lives in Guangzhou.

WANG Yuefei, *1956 in Guangzhou, lives in Shenzhen.

WONG Imaya, *1975 in Kuala Lumpur, lives in Kuala Lumpur Malaysia.

XIA Wenxi, *1979 in Xi'an, lives in Shenzhen.

YANG Zhen, *1973 in Prov. Henan, lives in Shenzhen.

YE Changchun, *1975 in Jiangxi, lives in Ningbo.

YU Ming-Lung, *1957 in Taipei, lives in Taipei Taiwan.

ZHANG Wanbao, *1981 in Shandong, lives in Shanghai.

ZHAO Qing, *1965 in Nanjing, lives in Nanjing.

Bibliografie (Auswahl)
Bibliography (selection)

Minick, Scott und Jiao Ping, *Chinese Graphic Design in the Twentieth Century*, London 1990.

IdN, International designers Network bimonthly digital design magazine, seit 1992.

Tai-keung, Kan, «Hong Kong», in: *Who's Who in Graphic Design*, Zürich 1994.

Van der Sanden, Michel, «Business, medicine, tha law... or design», in: *eye*, 17, Summer 1995.

Graphic Design in China '96, Shenzhen 1996.

von Kraft, Perdita (Hg.), *Plakate in China*, Brandenburgische Kunstsammlungen Cottbus, Cottbus 1997.

Escande, Yolande et al., «Signes de Chine», in: *étapes graphiques*, Nr. 34, 1997.

Chen, Chin-Lien und Chris Vermaas, «Travelogue: China, Hong Kong, Taiwan», in: *eye*, Nr. 28, Summer 1998.

The Outstanding Posters of 70th Founding Anniversary of China Academy of Fine Arts, CAFA, Beijing 1998.

International Fashion and Culture Poster Exhibition (The 1st International Poster Biennial), Ningbo 1999.

Shanghai International Invitational Poster exhibition, Shanghai 1999.

China Design Yearbook 2000–2001, Beijing 2001.

The International Poster Exhibition, Ningbo 2001; 2003; 2004. http://www.igdb-ningbo.com

Wong, Wendy Siuyi, «Detachment and Unification: A Chinese Graphic Design History in Greater China Since 1979», in: *Design Issues*, Vol. 17, Nr. 4, Dezember 2001.

Choko, Marc H. (Hg.), *L'affiche chinoise*, 1921–2001, Centre de design de l'Université du Québec à Montréal 2001.

Kristahn, Heinz-Jürgen (Hg.), *Das Avantgarde Plakat aus China, Spiegelbild der Öffentlichkeit*, Berlin 2001.

Wong, Wendy Siuyi, «In Search of a New Graphic Design Frontier in China: Establishing the "Chinese-ness" of International Style», 2002.
http://www.idemployee.id.tue.nl/g.w.m.rauterberg/conferences/CD_doNotOpen/ADC/final_paper/081.pdf

Zhao Yan (Hg.), *Contemporary design in China – 100 posters*, exhibition catalogue, Hangzhou 2002.

China International Poster Biennal, Hangzhou 2003; 2005.

Baur, Ruedi, Michel Bouvet, Yolande Escande et al., «Transitions Chinoises», in: *étapes graphiques*, Nr. 108, 2004.

Ecole nationale supérieure des arts décoratifs, *ENSAD* (Hg.), Hangzhou – Paris, Paris 2005.

Posters Lucerne (Hg.), *Bilder Schrift, zeitgenössische chinesische Schriftplakate*, Luzern 2005.

Peters, Robert L., «No Sleeping Dragon: The dawn of graphic design in China«, in: *Communication Arts*, 2006.
http://www.commarts.com/ca/feaint/china/113_china.html

Dank/Thanks
Urs Strähl, Hochschule für Gestaltung und Kunst Luzern, Fachbereich Grafik.

Eva Lüdi Kong, geboren 1968, in Biel, Schweiz. Grundstudium der Sinologie an der Universität Zürich, anschliessend Studium der Kalligrafie und Druckgrafik an der China Academy of Fine Arts, M.-A.-Studium der klassischen chinesischen Literatur an der Zhejiang University in Hangzhou (VR China). Seit 1992 tätig als Dolmetscherin und Übersetzerin im Bereich zeitgenössischer chinesischer Kunst und Literatur. Gleichzeitig Fotodokumentationen über die Entwicklung der chinesischen Städte und über Schriftzeichen im Stadtbild. Wohnt und arbeitet in Hangzhou (VR China).

Eva Lüdi Kong, born in 1968 in Biel, Switzerland. Basic course in Chinese Studies at Zurich University, then studied calligraphy and printed graphics at the China Academy of Fine Arts, M.A. in classical Chinese literature at Zhejiang University in Hangzhou (PR China). Has worked in the field of contemporary Chinese art and literature as an interpreter and translator since 1992, simultaneously preparing a photographic record of the development of Chinese cities and written characters in the cityscape. Lives and works in Hangzhou (PR China).

He Jianping, geboren 1973 in Fuyang, Prov. Zhejiang (VR China). 1991–1995 Grafik-Design Studium an der Hangzhou China Academy of Art. 1997–2000 Studium der Bildenden Kunst und ein Meisterschülerstudium an der Hochschule der Künste Berlin. Seit 2000 Künstlerischer Mitarbeiter an der Universität der Künste Berlin. Eigenes Studio «hesign» in Berlin seit 2002 und in Shanghai seit 2005.

He Jianping, born in 1973 in Fuyang, Zhejiang Province (PR China). Studied graphic design at the Hangzhou China Academy of Art, from1991–1995. Studied Fine Art and completed a master-pupil study at the Universität der Künste Berlin from1997–2000. Art assistant at the Universität der Künste Berlin from 2000. Own "hesign" studio in Berlin from 2002 and in Shanghai from 2005.

«Poster Collection»
Herausgegeben von/Published by
Felix Studinka
Kurator der Plakatsammlung
Curator of the Poster Collection
Museum für Gestaltung Zürich
In Zusammenarbeit mit/in cooperation with
Bettina Richter, Wissenschaftliche Mitarbeiterin/
Scientific collaborator
Christina Reble, Publikationen/Publications
Museum für Gestaltung Zürich

Typo China
Idee und Logistik/Idea and logistics: He Jianping, Berlin/Shanghai
Konzept, Redaktion/Concept, Editing:
Felix Studinka, Christina Reble
Gestaltung/Design: Integral Lars Müller
Übersetzung/Translation: Michael Robinson, London
Chinesische Bildlegenden/Chinese Captions:
Christof von Waldkirch, Zürich
Lithografie/Repro: Ast & Jakob, Vetsch AG, Köniz
Druck/Printing: Konkordia GmbH, Bühl/Bd.
Einband/Binding:
Josef Spinner Grossbuchbinderei GmbH, Ottersweier

© 2006
Hochschule für Gestaltung und Kunst Zürich, zfh
Museum für Gestaltung Zürich
Lars Müller Publishers

All rights reserved

Museum für Gestaltung Zürich
Plakatsammlung/Poster Collection
Limmatstrasse 57
CH–8005 Zürich/Switzerland
plakat.sammlung@museum-gestaltung.ch
www.museum-gestaltung.ch

Lars Müller Publishers
CH–5400 Baden/Switzerland
books@lars-muller.ch
www.lars-muller-publishers.com

ISBN 13: 978-3-03778-078-7
ISBN 10: 3-03778-078-9
Erste Auflage/First Edition 2006

Printed in Germany

apg Affichage